CRIMINAL RECORDS

Also edited by Anne Harvey

FACES IN A CROWD: POEMS ABOUT PEOPLE
OF CATERPILLARS, CATS AND CATTLE

for
SCOTT CHERRY
for all sorts of reasons
with love

Steal not this book for fear of shame,
For in it is the owner's name,
And when you die the Lord will say
'Where is that book you stole away?'

Then, if you say you do not know,
The Lord will say 'Go down below!'
But if you say you cannot tell
The Lord will say 'Oh, go to H—!'

Anon.

Criminal Records

Edited by Anne Harvey

Illustrated by Peter Viccars

VIKING

VIKING

Published by the Penguin Group
Penguin Books Ltd, 27 Wrights Lane, London W8 5TZ, England
Penguin Books USA Inc., 375 Hudson Street, New York, New York 10014, USA
Penguin Books Australia Ltd, Ringwood, Victoria, Australia
Penguin Books Canada Ltd, 10 Alcorn Avenue, Toronto, Ontario, Canada M4V 3B2
Penguin Books (NZ) Ltd, 182–190 Wairau Road, Auckland 10, New Zealand

Penguin Books Ltd, Registered Offices: Harmondsworth, Middlesex, England

First published 1994
1 3 5 7 9 10 8 6 4 2

Filmset in Ehrhardt by Selwood Systems, Midsomer Norton

Made and printed in Great Britain by Butler & Tanner Ltd, Frome and London

A CIP catalogue record for this book is available from the British Library

ISBN 0-670-85079-9

CONTENTS

MURDER MOST FOUL

DOING TIME

ROGUE'S GALLERY

INTRODUCTION

Breakfast time. I open a newspaper. Headlines jump out at me. CRIME INCREASE NATIONWIDE ... YOUNG THIEVES LAUGH AT LAW ... MUGGER POUNCES ON COLLEGE LECTURER ... THUGS SHOVE ELDERLY WOMAN TO GROUND ... DRUGS SEIZED IN SUBURBAN HOUSE ... NINE-YEAR-OLD SUSPECTED OF ARSON ... HOW TO SAVE OUR CHILDREN FROM CRIME ... Special Report ... page 15.

I turn to page 15 and read an alarming report on the rise in crime. One committed every six seconds ... Every six seconds? Surely when I began this anthology, it was one every three minutes? ... I pour a second cup of coffee and turn on the radio. ... THE RISE IN CRIME ... announces the newsreader ... IS REACHING ALARMING FIGURES ... I switch off and turn to my completed manuscript. ... With its assortment of poems on thieves and vandals, forgers and murderers, policemen and detectives, judges and accused, it lies innocently on the table next to the toast.

Poems about crime can't provide the answer to the rise in crime, but perhaps they can heighten our awareness and widen our understanding. For me, poetry has always done that. As I read hundreds of poems for the book, I came closer to the feelings of both criminal and victim, and thought more about background and motive, anticipation, guilt and punishment. Some of the poems painfully recall events that have touched us deeply. Some, set in the past, are distanced from our emotional involvement. Some, you may find surprising, are written with humour. The mood suddenly changes, the tension relaxes in a collection that has a serious intention, and will, I hope, provoke discussion. Always it is the poet's skill in handling a particular style that counts.

Take theft, for instance. There is an uneasy, sinister feeling to the way the Victorian American poet, Emily Dickinson, describes a house:

> Where two could creep
> One – hand the tools –
> The other peep –

while Susan Hamlyn brings a gruesome jokiness to the events in 'Atilla Takes a Hand'.

And murder: the cold-blooded phone box killing in Edward Lloyd's poem leaves a nasty taste, but we can't help laughing at Harry Graham's four-liner about the man who slew his wife ... 'because he had to stop her snoring'.

Crime has always been deplored and always of immense interest; the fascination for it is timeless. In the past, crowds flocked to the scaffold to witness the execution of a notorious highwayman. Women wept as a handsome villain made a stirring, farewell speech. Ballads were sung and broadsheets printed to keep the public up to date with the latest lurid events.

Today we read the newspaper and listen to the news with distress. Yet the evening could find us curled up with the latest paperback thriller, or glued to an exciting murder story on TV. In the comfort of our homes, we enjoy some very uncomfortable situations ... we escape into the city underworld of tough cops and tough crooks, or the quiet country house where intriguing clues are unravelled by a genteel detective – and then we switch off.

Thinking of all this, I turn back to the pages of *Criminal Records*. Lines from poems jump out at me. THE BORSTAL BOY IS ON THE RUN ... I DIDN'T STEAL ANYTHING, HONEST ... GRAFFITI ON THE WALL ... BAG SNATCHING IN DUBLIN ... BABY DIES IN CUPBOARD ... And I think they read rather like this morning's news on radio, like the headlines in the daily paper.

Anne Harvey

Don't Get Into Trouble

Hard words at first and threat'ning words
That are but noisy breath,
May grow to clubs and naked swords,
To murder and to death.

Isaac Watts (1674–1748)

A SMALL SIN

A lad when at school one day stole a pin,
And said that no harm was in such a small sin,
He next stole a knife and said 'twas a trifle,
Next thing he did was pockets to rifle.
Next thing he did was a house to break in,
The next thing – upon a gallows to swing!
So let us avoid ALL LITTLE SINNINGS
Since such is the end of petty beginnings.

Anon.

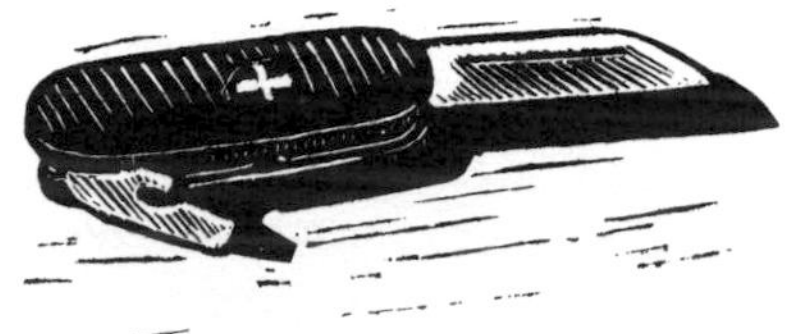

PLAYTIME

The simple guns have nothing to pretend.
We go to bed at eight, each night the same.
Over abandoned toys our mothers bend.

All that is broken let our fathers mend.
What leaves the nursery that we can't reclaim?
The simple guns have nothing to pretend.

This boy, who fires the match-sticks, is my friend.
We don't admit the accidental flame.
Over abandoned toys our mothers bend.

His rash intention is what I intend.
We knew each other the first time he came.
The simple guns have nothing to pretend.

But our pretence is why our people send
each to the other's house. We play their game.
Over abandoned toys our mothers bend.

It's anybody's guess how this will end.
Each time we say 'hello' we're taking aim.
The simple guns have nothing to pretend.
Over abandoned toys our mothers bend.

John Mole

BATMAN

Batman
Age 10½
Patrols the streets of his suburb
At night
Between 7 and 8 o'clock,
If he is out later than this
he is spanked
and sent to bed
Without supper.

Batman
Almost 11
Patrols the streets of his suburb
At night
After he has finished his homework.

Batman,
His freckles
And secret identity
Protected
By the mask and cloak
His Auntie Elsie
Made on her sewing machine,
Patrols
At night
Righting Wrongs.

Tonight he is on the trail of
Raymond age 11
(large for his age)
Who has stolen Stephen's
Gobstoppers and football cards.

Batman
Patrolling the streets of his suburb
Righting Wrongs
Finds Raymond,
Demands the return of the stolen goods.
Raymond knocks him over,
Rips his mask,
Tears his cloak,
And steals his utility belt.
Batman starts to cry,
Wipes his eyes with his cape
(His hankie was in the belt).

Next day
Auntie Elsie says
This is the 14th time
I've had to mend your
Batman costume.
If it happens again
You'll have to whistle for it.

Batman
Eats a bag of crisps.

Martyn Wiley

WARNING TO PARENTS

Save them from terror; do not let them see
The ghost behind the stairs, the hidden crime.
They will, no doubt, grow out of this in time
And be impervious as you and me.

Be sure there is a night-light close at hand;
The plot of that old film may well come back,
The ceiling, with its long, uneven crack,
May hint at things no child can understand.

You do all this and are surprised one day
When you discover how the child can gloat
On Belsen and on tortures – things remote
To him. You find it hard to watch him play

With thoughts like these, and find it harder still
To think back to the time when you also
Caught from the cruel past a childish glow
And felt along your veins the wish to kill.

Fears are more personal than we had guessed –
We only need ourselves; time does the rest.

Elizabeth Jennings

BYE-CHILD

*He was discovered in the henhouse
where she had confined him. He was
incapable of saying anything.*

When the lamp glowed,
A yolk of light
In their back window,
The child in the outhouse
Put his eye to a chink –

Little henhouse boy,
Sharp-faced as new moons
Remembered, your photo still
Glimpsed like a rodent
On the floor of my mind,

Little moon man,
Kennelled and faithful
At the foot of the yard,
Your frail shape, luminous,
Weightless, is stirring the dust,

The cobwebs, old droppings
Under the roosts
And dry smells from scraps
She put through your trapdoor
Morning and evening.

After those footsteps, silence;
Vigils, solitudes, fasts,
Unchristened tears,
A puzzled love of the light.
But now you speak at last

With a remote mime
Of something beyond patience,
Your gaping wordless proof
Of lunar distances
Travelled beyond love.

Seamus Heaney

— EDDY SCOTT GOES OUT — TO PLAY

Outside, the street is dark with rain,
The arcade is brightly lit with screens;
Eddy feeds his dinner money
To hypnotizing fruit machines.

'Don't get into trouble,
Don't talk to funny men,
Here's a pound to buy your dinner.'
Eddy's left alone again.

The coins clunk down, the fruit rolls round
The bright lights flash like mad,
Then disappear like the dinner
Eddy hadn't had.

Eddy's mum's at work all day,
Eddy's dad has gone away.
Hot or cold, wet or fine,
Eddie Scott's sent out to play.

The money's gone. No food to eat.
Eddy checks round all the trays
In case somebody's missed a coin.
'No money, sonny?' someone says.

'Don't get into trouble,
Don't talk to funny men,
Here's a pound to buy your dinner.'
Eddy's left alone again.

'I'll lend you money if you like,
Or how about some sweets?
I've seen you here and there before,
Wandering round the streets.'

Eddy's mum's at work all day,
Eddy's dad has gone away.
Hot or cold, wet or fine,
Eddie Scott's sent out to play.

'Would you like a slap-up meal?
You would? Get in the car,
I'll take you to a place I know
That isn't very far.'

'Don't get into trouble,
Don't talk to funny men,
Here's a pound to buy your dinner.'
Eddy's left alone again.

Mum gets home at six o'clock,
'Eddy, are you home?' she'll call.
There'll be no answer: just her voice
Echoing along the hall.

Eddy's mum's at work all day,
Eddy's dad has gone away.
Hot or cold, wet or fine,
Eddie was sent out to play.

David Orme

THE BORSTAL BOY

This boy has broken out of that
odd public school by name Borstal.
The police are after him and when
they get him he'll know what's what.

The Borstal Boy is on the run.
He really thinks that he can hide
in a ditch by an open field.
He does not know what he has done.

He has red hair and thinks he can
talk sensibly to cows and horses.
Why? He trusts them. He trusts tractors. He
does not trust his fellow man.

The police claim he stole a car.
He has a way with old machines.
He does not know the arm of the law
can reach very fast and far.

He sleeps almost every night in a
corrugated-covered ditch.
He keeps a twenty-two air rifle.
He shoots pheasants for his dinner.

The parson does his simple best
to talk him into going back
to Borstal but the boy can not
perceive the need for his arrest.

I saw him yesterday beside
the river, stalking with his gun
a pheasant gaudy as a prince.
I heard it shriek out as it died.

George Barker

FORM PHOTOGRAPH No. 29

The man of the family, who swears at his widowed mother
And smokes in the house. She appeals to the Staff for help
On Parents' Evening, in tears, for the character-training
Of caning, lines and keeping-in after school,
And in his cowardly way he comes to heel;
But falls deadweight on her or anyone
Soft enough not to stand up to him,
Opening locker doors in smaller boys' faces
And shutting desklids on their heads and fingers.

Stanley Cook

POCKET MONEY

'I can't explain what happens to my cash,'
I can, but can't – not to my Mum and Dad.
'Give us 10p or get another bash' –

That's where it goes. And though their questions crash
Like blows, and though they're getting mad,
I can't explain what happens to my cash;

How can I tell the truth? I just rehash
Old lies. The others have and I'm the had:
'Give us 10p or get another bash.'

'For dinner, Dad? . . . Just sausages and mash.'
'That shouldn't make you broke by Wednesday, lad.'
I can't explain. What happens to my cash? –

My friends all help themselves. I get the ash
Of fags I buy and give, get none. 'Too bad.
Give us 10p or get another bash

For being you.' And still I feel the thrash
Of stronger, firmer hands than mine; the sad
Disgust of living like a piece of trash.
I can't explain what happens to my cash.
'Give us 10p or get another bash.'

Mick Gowar

THE PURSE

I pinched it from my mother's purse,
Pretending it's a game.
My muscles tightened: hard and tense.
I pinched it just the same.

'I need it as a loan,' I said,
'It's not against the law.'
'I won't do it again,' I said.
I've said all that before.

The reason was the cash at first,
It isn't any more;
I do it . . . well, because I do,
I don't know what it's for.

I only know that when the house
Is silent, empty, still,
I head towards my parents' room
As if against my will.

The sweat is cold upon my neck,
My back and arms feel strange,
I'm sure that someone's watching me
As I pick out her change.

But no one ever catches me,
Sometimes I wish they would;
Then perhaps I'd stop and think
And give it up for good.

But my mum trusts me, buys me
  things:
Each kindness makes it worse
Because I know, when she's next door,
My hands will find her purse.

David Kitchen

EDDY'S FIRE

All summer
Eddy had been threatening a fire
threatening to set the woods alight
so the sky would become a firework
spelling his name

and one hot restless day
I saw the smoke curling over the common
Eddy had started his fire.

'Stop' I shouted
seeing the one tree blaze.
I rushed to the one telephone box
they hadn't ripped
and dialled 999.

It was my first time.

When I got back –
to tell them to hide –
I found they'd put the fire out.

'I've called the fire brigade' I said
'I've dialled 999'
and my words were scared wet twigs
I could not rub together

Like Sir Walter Raleigh
stretching out his cloak for the Queen
Eddy threw the rest of his petrol can
and Nick gave up his last lighted fag

And for me
the trees roared like giant ovens
and because of me the leaves burned
and the bushes joined red hot hands
and danced in time to the sirens

'Are you the little girl who called us?'
asked the Fire Brigade.
'You've saved a lot of damage.

There's terrible vandalism in this area.'

Valerie Sinason

A COFFEE HOUSE

A little boy of twenty months. He fits
  Exactly into space and floor.
He runs a few yards as his mother sits
Talking but she's soon after him. What's more

She wears an anxious frown. He's full of glee
  Not knowing how we all
Share in watching over him while he
Laughs loudly. He knows that he will not fall

Although he hasn't moved about for long.
  Fair hair, a smile of grace.
If he knew one he'd sing a morning call
But there is worry on each watching face,

For this year one horrific murder was
  Done by two boys of ten
Our minds are full of that and all its loss.
When shall we laugh *with* children once again?

Elizabeth Jennings

The Devil Is Boredom

Everywhere they were waiting. In silence.
In boredom. Staring into space.
Reflecting on nothing, or on violence
That is long since past. Wondering,
Wondering what will happen next.
They are waiting. . . .

from STREET GANG, *H. Webster (20th Century)*

– A HOLBORN LAMPPOST –

I'm half-way down a Holborn lamppost
with the warm bulb in my hand.
I'm barefoot for the chimpanzee grip.
Imagine a warm night in October,
a couple of quarts of special bitter
then the mischievous gambol home.
My bushy cousin is on the pavement –
an accomplice, a lookout is needed.
A big boy, he is fair at rugby
and a rare hand at the double-bass.
I'm stationary, taking a breather,
considering the lure of Tandoori smells.
My cousin raises his whisper, points
to the corner where a cop is hiding,
peeking round, blue hat in his hand.
He's like that, my Yorkshire cousin.
A plane whines above me, heading west.
I'm twenty tomorrow, at 3 a.m.,
and finally I've a head for heights.
But perhaps it's time I slid down.

Matthew Sweeney

— I USED TO CLIMB — UP LAMPPOSTS, SIR

I used to climb up lampposts, sir,
At twelve o'clock at night.
I used to climb up lampposts, sir,
I knew it wasn't right.
I used to climb up lampposts, sir,
But now I've seen the light.

Colin West

LOCAL MYSTERY

I'm the one who places
traffic cones on top of bus shelters
It doesn't mean anything
but it provokes letters to newspapers

It's me that's responsible
for decapitating belisha beacons
leaving their souls beating and blinking
at the panther-black night

I confess. I drop ice-cream
on the station concourse
That activity is not deliberate
merely flustered

I also remove strategic railings from public parks
this is my service to the weary

When drunk, and swaying like a flamingo on a skateboard,
I hurl silver helmets of beanshoots
at the whirlpool pavement

I discard shopping trolleys
upturned refugees in bushes
pleading for repatriation

I walk past you daily
I have various shapes
changeable expressions

I hang upside down from motorway bridges
composing slogans against oppression
One day I will write what I mean
it will say 'Notice me'
but I don't think anyone will.

Stewart Henderson

— WE DON'T WANT IT GREY —

Graffiti on the wall, graffiti on
the train, graffiti on the city street,
graffiti on your brain. Write on! There's no-
where sacred, it's a technicolour show.
Write on whatever's ugly, let the con-
crete glow. Paint your words with music, beat

your techno-pop, electro-funk your ma-
ma, rap the world: hip-hop. Across the earth
one nation, dancing through the town, and chant-
ing songs and poetry, with words you can't
put down. The brothers and the sisters, the fa-
mily of man, it's gonna be the birth-

time of the spraying-can. Graffiti on
the arms, graffiti on the face of Babylon!

Norman Silver

from UNLUCKY FOR SOME

I'm no good, that's what I've been told
ever since I can remember. So
I try to live up to my reputation.
Or down to it. Thievin mainly.
And drugs. You get used to prison.
Don't like it though, being cooped up.
That's why I couldn't work in a shop
or a factory. Drive me crazy.
Can't settle down. 21 years old
and I look 40. It's the drugs.
I'll O.D. probably. Couldn't care less.
Rather die young than grow old.
I'm no good, that's what I've been told.

Roger McGough

— THE VICTIM DIED — OF STAB WOUNDS

It was when the novelty of life
Wore off he bought a flick-knife;
And the leather jacket he stole
Because it was a status symbol
That helped him to play it cool,
To prove he was nobody's fool.

Then he ganged up. He was only
Doing what insecure, lonely
Types do, as the psychiatrist
Pointed out. Put to the test,
He had no option but to climb
The ladder of petty crime.

What's more vulnerable than age?
A man counting dough in his
  dotage,
Before the shop door shuts,
Asks for it. But it takes guts
To grab the loot and scarper
Under the busy nose of a copper.

You don't expect old men to show
Fight, to bellow, to blow
A referee's whistle. It's a life
For a life. The flick-knife
Burns in the sweating palm
Of the hand that means no harm.

It's that simple. As for death,
What is it? You buy a wreath,
Pull down a blind, drink a pint
In memory of some old skinflint,
Then put it out of your mind
Until you next pull down a blind.

A death is a natural thing. A killing
Is a special sort of thing.
The slob had let him down by
  dying;
He lay there not even trying
To live. The flick-knife stuck
Out of him. What bloody luck!

It's the enormity of the offence
Proves, in a way, its innocence.
Not that this helped him much
Before the Bench. He lost touch
Somehow with himself. Disgrace
Stamped on a magistrate's face

Didn't register. What maybe did
Was the shock of the blood
Trickling slowly into a crack.
If he could, he would have put it
  back
Into the body. That he never can
Makes him, prematurely, a man.

F. Pratt-Green

THE STUFF

We'd heard all the warnings; knew its nicknames.
It arrived in our town by word of mouth
and crackled like wildfire through the grapevine
of gab and gossip. It came from the south

so we shunned it, naturally;
sent it to Coventry

and wouldn't have touched it with a barge pole
if it hadn't been at the club one night.
Well, peer group pressure and all that twaddle
so we fussed around it like flies round shite

and watched,
and waited

till one kid risked it, stepped up and licked it
and came from every pore in his body.
That clinched it. It snowballed; whirlpooled. Listen,
no one was more surprised than me to be

cutting it, mixing it,
snorting and sniffing it

or bulking it up with scouring powder
or chalk, or snuff, or sodium chloride
and selling it under the flyover.
At first we were laughing. It was all right

to be drinking it, eating it,
living and breathing it

but things got seedy; people went missing.
One punter surfaced in the ship-canal
having shed a pair of concrete slippers.
Others were bundled into the back of vans

and were quizzed, thumped,
finished off and dumped

or vanished completely like Weldon Kees:
their cars left idle under the rail bridge
with its cryptic hoarding which stumped the police:
'Oldham – Home of the tubular bandage.'

Others were strangled.
Not that it stopped us.

Someone bubbled us. CID sussed us
and found some on us. It was cut and dried.
They dusted, booked us, cuffed us and pushed us
down to the station and read us our rights.

Possession and supplying:
we had it, we'd had it.

In Court I ambled up and took the oath
and spoke the addict's side of the story.
I said grapevine, barge pole, whirlpool, chloride,
concrete, bandage, station, story. Honest.

Simon Armitage

Weldon Kees, the American poet, vanished on
18 July 1955, abandoning his car on the
approach to the Golden Gate Bridge,
San Francisco.

ATTENDING A FOOTBALL MATCH

It sneaked past watchful attendants,
warned to be on the look-out for It
among the male together-noise.
White faces on dark clothes
cohered, shading the terracing
to the anonymous crouch of a crowd.

The ninepin players trotted in.
Kinetic muscles in play,
and Matt, John, Jock and Wullie
bounced on their excitement's cheers.

But as the ball began to score
goals spent in a stretched net,
It wedged Itself between the roars
of the single-backed, two-minded thing,
for *game*, insinuated *name*,
a syllableless, faceless feeling
of nothing words identified.

Then suddenly It broke loose –
bottles hit fists and screams.
Police tore the crowd apart
to get It. It eluded them.

From spectators crushed by shock,
a swearing vanful of louts,
the cut-up quiet in hospitals,
no real evidence could be taken.
Charges were, of course, preferred –
disorderly conduct, obstructing the police –
but no one found out what It was,
or whose It is, or where It came from.

Maurice Lindsay

BEHIND THE STORY

'He must have been doing eighty up behind,'
The old man says. 'I couldn't get out of the way.'
'A bee hit me smack in the eye. I was blind,'
Is all the leathered, zippered youth can say.
'I couldn't see this joker round the bend.'

The girl who once had been a passenger
Lies on the grass under a coat, not caring,
Suddenly dead. Nearby, a part of her,
Still in the bloody shoe she had been wearing,
Begins to cool. It will be looked for later.

The old man simply stands. The back of his car
Is concave now, the window dark and yawning.
He vaguely wonders where his glasses are,
Why the worst horrors always give least warning,
Hears something somewhere dripping on hot tar.

'If this old devil hadn't been bloody crawling
I'd probably have missed him.' Now excuses
Come to the young imagination, falling
Out of the desperate air; these the tongue uses,
Trying to minimize, cushion the appalling.

The dazed old man says nothing; watches sadly
While measurements are taken; wonders why
Accidents happen. He was not driving badly!
Unfair as it is he cannot ever deny
His thirty made the youth's shrill eighty deadly.

They will cart her off to a slab, the girl who is dead –
Her and the part of her – and attempt to make
The face presentable to be identified.
Next week the youth will talk of a new bike;
Brash again, say to his cronies, 'That old sod
Was too old to drive. He shouldn't be on the road.'

Eric Millward

DARE DEVIL

The Devil is boredom – you know, nowt-to-do;
is all the fancy things on telly you can't have
and all those smarm-bags enjoying them; is
a classy car shining in the car park, alone,
like a bird you fancy giving the come-on. And
the Devil's that rich-bastard owner knocking back
shorts on expenses. And there are other Devils
to dare: the horror of concrete, the scraggy estate,
hot squealing tyres, the glare in the eyes
of the kid at the wheel hot out of Hell,
glass that is shattered and buckled metals,
broken bones and crimson steaming blood

Matt Simpson

EDUCATION FOR LEISURE

Today I am going to kill something. Anything.
I have had enough of being ignored and today
I am going to play God. It is an ordinary day,
a sort of grey with boredom stirring in the streets.

I squash a fly against the window with my thumb.
We did that at school. Shakespeare. It was in
another language and now the fly is in another language.
I breathe out talent on the glass to write my name.

I am a genius. I could be anything at all, with half
the chance. But today I am going to change the world.
Something's world. The cat avoids me. The cat
knows I am a genius and has hidden itself.

I pour the goldfish down the bog. I pull the chain.
I see that it is good. The budgie is panicking.
Once a fortnight, I walk the two miles into town
for signing on. They don't appreciate my autograph.

There is nothing left to kill. I dial the radio
and tell the man he's talking to a superstar.
He cuts me off. I get our bread-knife and go out.
The pavements glitter suddenly. I touch your arm.

Carol Ann Duffy

Sneaking Up The Stair

No, I had set no prohibiting sign,
And yes, my land was hardly fenced,
Nevertheless the land was mine:
I was being trespassed on and against

from Trespassing, *Robert Frost (1874–1963)*

RUMOUR

Somebody is whispering on the stair.
What are those words half spoken, half drawn back?
Whence are those muffled words, some red, some black?
Who is whispering? Who is there?

Somebody is sneaking up the stair,
His feet approaching every doorway,
Yet never a moment standing anywhere.

Now many whisper close outside some door.
O suddenly push it open wide.
You see: whoever said he heard them, he has lied.

And yet words are left dark like heavy dust
In many rooms, or red on iron like rust:
And who contrives to leave them? Someone must.

In every street, this noisy town of ours
Has stealthy whispering watchers walking round,
Recording all our movements, every sound,
Hissing and shuffling, and they may have found
Today my name: tomorrow they'll find yours.

Harold Monro

PEEPING TOM

He taps on their window
as the lights go out;
his fingers are sparrows' claws,
his face, bloated against
the window-glass is moon-white,
spread-lipped. He makes marks:
nose blot, lip print, grease,
no fingers. Fear feathers
through the flat, feeds him:
he is alive, noticeable.
They are helpless to do
other than wait or move,
whatever they choose
he has made them.

Lois Beeson

THE HOUSE-WRECKERS

The house-wreckers have left the door and a staircase,
now leading to the empty room of night.

Charles Reznikoff

BURGLARY

He came, took nothing, but only scraps such as
waste-paper, half-eaten fruit and only a shoe.
What did he think seeing this picture? One book
is on the chair. He must have read. Thought what?
I see his finger-prints on the cutlery; the stove
is still hot. He must have cooked. And eaten. And
leaving, he left no dead leaf on the garden path.

He comes, takes almost everything and leaves nothing
but only scraps, such as waste-paper and only a shoe.
That picture is gone and all the books. What happens
then, if he changes his mind and brings them back?
Even if not, the policy will cover the loss, nothing
was after all irreplaceable. Buy new things. Furnish
the rooms. Build a new fire. And thank God.

He will come, will take nothing that the policy covers.
Hungry to take away, he will take away what
remained unnoticed, unprofitable and I
will lose. He must not come. Although hidden,
his deft eyes may see what enemies do not,
what friends cannot think of seeing. That he must not
burgle. I shall prepare for him a marvellous trap.

Taner Baybars

OF DOGS AND THIEVES

To keep thieves by night out of my house,
I keep dogs to aid me in my yard,
Whose barking at stir of every mouse,
By lack of sleep killeth me in regard –
Thieves or dogs then, which may best be spared?
Murder is the most mischief here to guess;
Thieves can do no more, and dogs will do no less.

John Heywood

THE VILLAGE BURGLAR

Under a spreading chestnut tree the village burglar lies,
The burglar is a hairy man with whiskers round his eyes
And the muscles of his brawny arms keep off the little flies.

He goes on Sunday to the church to hear the Parson shout.
He puts a penny in the plate and takes a pound note out
And drops a conscience-stricken tear in case he is found out.

Anon.

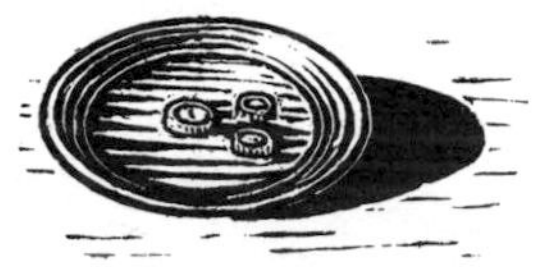

THE TIDY BURGLAR

The burglar tip-toed across the lawn
That was cut like a carpet, sprinkler-smooth,
Past ornamental waterfall
And pale blue utterly algae-free pool,

Crossed the patio, brushed through vines
Dripping with bunches of ripe, black grapes,
Cracked a window, stepped inside,
Admired the decanters, the velvet drapes,

Examined the stereo, touched the pictures,
Feeling the texture of the jagged oil-paint,
Opened a cabinet with Georgian silver
And Tudor miniatures in intricate frames,

But took nothing. He went upstairs
To the master-bedroom's jewellery cases:
A diamond collar, six rings, a rare
Black pearl, some rubies, a dozen bracelets.

His eye strayed to the rumpled bed.
Untidiness always drove him frantic.
He made it neatly, stacked cushions at the head.
Then, hearing a noise, left empty-handed.

Leo Aylen

THE SPOONS

One day
After a bout of how-any-son-of-mine
I took the spoons
Some knives and a fork from home
And left a note for Mum
And came away
To a furnished room.

Mum was so mad
About the cutlery
She pinned the blame
On her son-in-law
(My sister's old man)
On the floor below
She had the police come in
Bit of a shame
But how should I know
What a woman like that will do
When she's been had?

Anyway, I had paid
Over the years, for these spoons.

Never a word since then
Exchanged between son and Mum
Seven years now gone by
In a furnished room
Sometimes I wonder whether
She ever misses me
Or at least my salary.

I have a drink and a laugh
Now and then, with my brother-in-
law.
He would have done the same,
He says, except for his wife.
They still live underneath

My mum, and she bangs at night
On the ceiling, and that's it.

No women in my life,
Peace, perfect peace,
In a furnished room
And the job is going all right

But I'd like to have seen her face
When she missed the spoons.

Elma Mitchell

WHAT HE TOOK

He took her fancy when he came
  He took her hand, he took a kiss:
He took no notice of the shame
  That glowed her happy cheek at this:
He took to coming afternoons:
  He took an oath he'd ne'er deceive:
He took her father's silver spoons,
  And after that he took his leave.

Anon.

— MAN IN HOTEL ROOM WITH STOLEN FORK —

The taxis circle
round the square
taking people from places
to places.

It's mid-December in WC1.
The day is over, the bulb lingers on.
Man in hotel fork with stolen room.

He stole the fork in a curry place,
now there's guilt written sweaty all over his face.
Man in stolen hotel room with fork.

In the hallway it's Christmas, on the stairs it's goodwill
as he forks in the meat and it makes him feel ill.
Man in stolen fork with hotel room.

He's sick in the basin, he's sick in the bin.
He's empty as history, lonely as sin.
Room in stolen man with hotel fork.

And the taxis circle
round the square
taking people from places
to places.

Ian McMillan

FOUR SEASONS

Now they've taken everything, you said,
camera, cassette-player, films, tapes, money.
At night you keep a knife beside your bed.

Love, we're horrified. All winter we've read
your letters and worried about security.
Now they've taken everything, you said

– including that Vivaldi you recorded
tape-to-tape at home last summer for me?
At night you keep a knife beside your bed.

What a year you're having: back here my head
sings with your music's verve and energy.
Now they've taken everything, you said.

Autumn in Africa then, red leaves grounded,
the fall. Strange to think that out there somebody –
at night you keep a knife beside your bed –

stoops and switches on and hears, instead
of envy, this clear spring called Vivaldi.
Now they've taken everything, you said.
At night you keep a knife beside your bed.

Hubert Moore

RUN

An angry shout snatched up my gaze
From among the shoppers to across the street
Where a jacketed man, tidy and grey,
Turned with heavy haste down a street that led
Away through silent cars and bending trees.
He ran and shouted hoarsely, for the running
Robbed him of his fury's voice.
Ahead of him, my sprinting eyes leapt
To where he strove to be
And saw, now fifty yards ahead,
A racing boy in joyous blue, moving as though
A turning key made clockwork motion
Of his smooth and perfect speed.
Under his arm, the proof of his purloining;
Above car roofs his thighs pedalled the air
And rode a pavement higher than the one I trod.
The man in grey gave up his chase
Despite his rage, before the boy in blue was out of sight.
And we who stood at the dull bus stop
And those who covered their mouths at the baker's door,
Stood doughy, heavy with awakening and shock.
I, though wincing for the man in grey,
Robbed and shaken on such an ordinary day,
Stood printing and reprinting in my mind
Each new, still instant of a perfect human run.

Susan Hamlyn

SHOPLIFTING

'I dare you!'
  says a little voice
  soft and sly and very wicked.

'You can show them
  you ain't chicken
  you ain't yeller

– Are you? Are you?'

'I dare you!'
  says a little voice
  from deep inside.

'Show them all that
  you're a man
  you're tough and hard

– You can do it! You can do it!'

'I dare you!'
  says the little voice.
  'It's easy, anyone can do it

Show them what you're made of –
  – Quick! Now!
                Do it! Do it! Do it! Do it!'

Mick Gowar

THE MAN WHO FINDS HIS SON HAS BECOME A THIEF

Coming into the store at first angry
At the accusation, believing in
The word of his boy who has told him:
I didn't steal anything, honest.

Then becoming calmer, seeing that anger
Will not help in the business, listening painfully
As the other's evidence unfolds, so painfully slow.

Then seeing gradually that evidence
Almost as if tighten slowly around the neck
Of his son, at first vaguely circumstantial, then gathering
damage
Until there is present the unmistakable odour of guilt
Which seeps now into the mind and lays its poison.

Suddenly feeling sick and alone and afraid,
As if an unseen hand had slapped him in the face
For no reason whatsoever; wanting to get out
Into the street, the night, the darkness, anywhere to hide
The pain that must show in the face to these strangers, the
fear.

It must be like this.
It could hardly be otherwise.

Raymond Souster

SUGAR AND CREAM

To the Pick-Your-Own near Bath
come Charles and Marjorie Plunkett-Lord
with sun-hats, sticks and folding chairs
bought by a son who lives abroad.

Up and down the rows they go.
Beneath the leaves the strawberries gleam.
In their basket, two containers
one of sugar, one of cream.

They settle in a sunny spot
then get to work, a perfect team.
Charles, more agile, picks, while Marjorie
dips them in sugar, then in cream.

Into alternate mouths she pops them,
laughs, reliving love's young dream.
Watching from his till, the farmer's
swearing in a steady stream.

'Bloody hell! Those wrinklies! That's
enough to make a bloke blaspheme
– not only eating without paying
but bringing sugar! Bringing cream!'

'Look, I'm the owner and . . .' 'Oh, I'm so
awfully glad.' She gives a beam,
'We're frightfully grateful for your service,
your strawberries really are supreme!'

The farmer gulps. He feels embarrassed,
he's like an organ out of steam.
'My pleasure – er . . . do come next year
and bring your sugar and your cream.'

Carole Satyamurti

YOUNG THIEVES

The farmer must have returned
very suddenly. Anyway, we were all so busy
stripping his berry bushes the first warning we had
was his opening cannon's blast and the buckshot
whistling not too high above our heads.

He must have laughed himself silly
when he shuffled up to where we'd been picking,
and found the six-quart baskets nicely filled
to overflowing with the ripe red berries
we'd been too damned surprised and frightened
to take with us on our crazy, headlong flight
from an old man and his cockeyed shotgun.

Raymond Souster

FLOWER LOVER FINED $26

A 57-year-old man who described himself as a 'lover of flowers' was yesterday ordered to pay $26 for picking three roses from the Promenade Gardens.

The Court was told that Oscar Agard was seen picking the roses by a Town constable on duty in the Promenade Gardens.

Asked by Magistrate Rudolph Harper what he was going to do with the roses, Agard replied, 'Sir, I am a lover of flowers.' He was given two months to pay the fine.

not knowing the blood of flowers in their redtape veins
how could they understand his fingers' dream of roses
they who guard what they do not breathe or feel?

not knowing the pulse of petals in their clauses
neatly framed to cage a flower and her lover
how could they understand a worn man's need
for a moment's madness
shared gently with the listening rose?

John Agard

— ATTILA TAKES — A HAND

We drive through the gateway,
Get out of the car
And see to our horror
The door is ajar.

'My God! We've been burgled!
It's happened again!
Perhaps they're still in there?
Bad boys? Or tough men?

'But where is Attila?
Where *is* that beast?
We thought the Alsatian
Would scare them at least.

'Oh, here is the hero!
And wagging his tail!
Why didn't you give them
The CDs as well?

'Get back to the kitchen!
Guard dog indeed!
No one so cowardly
Should wear collar and lead!'

Attila slinks out
But then, strangely, lingers
And sniffs by his forepaw
Two fresh human fingers.

Susan Hamlyn

— I KNOW SOME LONELY — HOUSES

I know some lonely Houses off the Road
A Robber'd like the look of –
Wooden barred,
And Windows hanging low,
Inviting to –
A Portico,
Where two could creep –
One – hand the Tools –
The other peep –
To make sure All's Asleep –

Old fashioned eyes –
Not easy to surprise!

How orderly the Kitchen'd look, by
 night,
With just a Clock –
But they could gag the Tick –
And Mice won't bark –
And so the Walls – don't tell –
None – will –

A pair of Spectacles ajar just stir –
An Almanac's aware –
Was it the Mat – winked,
Or a Nervous Star?
The Moon – slides down the stair,
To see who's there!

There's plunder – where –
Tankard, or Spoon –
Earring – or Stone –
A Watch – Some Ancient Brooch
To match the Grandmama –
Staid sleeping – there –

Day – rattles – too
Stealth's – slow –
The Sun has got as far
As the third Sycamore –
Screams Chanticleer
'Who's there?'

And Echoes – Trains away,
Sneer – 'Where'!
While the old Couple, just astir,
Fancy the Sunrise – left the door ajar!

Emily Dickinson

MURDER MOST FOUL

Murder most foul, as in the best it is;
But this most foul, strange, and unnatural . . .

from HAMLET, *William Shakespeare (1564–1616)*

LONDON NIGHTS

Prepare for death if here at night you roam,
And sign your will before you sup from home.
  Some fiery fop, with new commission vain,
Who sleeps on brambles till he kills his man;
Some frolic drunkard, reeling from a feast,
Provokes a broil, and stabs you for a jest . . .
  In vain, these dangers past, your doors you close,
And hope the balmy blessings of repose;
Cruel with guilt, and daring with despair,
The midnight murd'rer bursts the faithless bar;
Invades the sacred hour of silent rest,
And leaves, unseen, a dagger in your breast.

Samuel Johnson

FROM MY NOTES FOR A SERIES OF LECTURES ON MURDER

It is not difficult to kill
Your enemy if you've sufficient will
But murderers are often in a hurry
And simply will not take the time to bury
The murderee. I'll indicate tomorrow
Just why this course is not for you to follow.

Stevie Smith

EDWARD

'How comes that blood all over your shirt?
My son, come tell it to me.'
'It's the blood of my little guinea pig –
O mother, please let me be.
It's the blood of my little guinea pig –
O mother, please let me be.'

'Your guinea pig's blood is not so red.
My son, come tell it to me.'
'It's the blood of my little hunting dog
That played in the field for me . . .'

'Your dog lies yonder, O my son,
And this it could not be.'
'It is the blood of my old roan horse
That pulled the plow for me . . .'

'How comes that blood all over your shirt?
My son, you must tell to me.'
'It's the blood of my little brother Bill
Who I killed in the field today . . .'

'And what will you do when your father comes home?
My son, come tell it to me.'
'I'll put my feet in the bottom of a boat
I'll put my feet in the bottom of a boat
And sail across the sea.
And sail across the sea.'

Anon.

— BRADY AT SADDLEWORTH — MOOR

Out, this is air, abrupt and everywhere,
the light and sky all one blaze of it.
Count them: eleven clear hours of wind
over the world's tops into my face –

this old bleached-out moon always adrift
through the bad dreams of the neighbourhood.
In my thousand days I count this day:
the moor, all its space and vastness

I hear them say I say. I find nothing
in all four corners of the wind
where stones haven't changed, tumps, gullies
one blue blur of heather and upland grass

where one grave looks much like another.
Think how many years the rain fell I felt
my heart in my chest a fist of sour dust
forming in the acids of my discontent.

But it knows one thought: nothing's forgot
though my vision's bad, my sanity debatable.
I can forget, I can remember, I can be mad,
I will never be as free again, ever.

Nor will anyone be free of me. Count on it.

Ken Smith

Ian Brady was found guilty on 6 May 1966 of killing three children. He was twenty-eight and his accomplice, Myra Hindley, twenty-three. Twenty-two years later they confessed to other killings, and the case known as the Moors Murders has never been forgotten.

MURDER IN THE RED BARN

So they hanged William Corder,
They hanged William Corder,
They hanged him up high
On a tall gallows tree

For he murdered his sweetheart,
The girl who had loved him,
And promised her falsely
His wife she should be.

So all you young people
Take heed of this story
Don't trifle with hearts
Or you may end the same . . .

And they'll hang you up high
Yes they'll high you up high,
To blow in the wind
On a tall gallows tree . . .

Anon.

William Corder was arrested for the murder of Maria Marten and hanged before an audience of 10,000 people in Bury St Edmunds, Suffolk, on 18 August 1828. His skeleton is still preserved, along with an account of the trial bound in his own skin. The rope with which he was hanged was sold at £1 an inch.

PORPHYRIA'S LOVER

The rain set early in tonight,
  The sullen wind was soon awake,
It tore the elm-tops down for spite,
  And did its worst to vex the lake:
  I listened with heart fit to break.
When glided in Porphyria; straight
  She shut the cold out and the storm,
And kneeled and made the cheerless grate
  Blaze up, and all the cottage warm;
  Which done, she rose, and from her form
Withdrew the dripping cloak and shawl,
  And laid her soiled gloves by, untied
Her hat and let the damp hair fall,
  And, last, she sat down by my side
  And called me. When no voice replied,
She put my arm about her waist,
  And made her smooth white shoulder bare,
And all her yellow hair displaced,
  And, stooping, made my cheek lie there,
  And spread, o'er all, her yellow hair,
Murmuring how she loved me – she
  Too weak, for all her heart's endeavour,
To set its struggling passion free
  From pride, and vainer ties dissever,
  And give herself to me for ever.
But passion sometimes would prevail,
  Nor could tonight's gay feast restrain
A sudden thought of one so pale
  For love of her, and all in vain:
  So, she was come through wind and rain.
Be sure I looked up at her eyes
  Happy and proud; at last I knew
Porphyria worshipped me; surprise
  Made my heart swell, and still it grew

While I debated what to do.
That moment she was mine, mine, fair,
Perfectly pure and good: I found
A thing to do, and all her hair
In one long yellow string I wound
Three times her little throat around,
And strangled her. No pain felt she;
I am quite sure she felt no pain.
As a shut bud that holds a bee,
I warily oped her lids: again
Laughed the blue eyes without a stain.
And I untightened next the tress
About her neck; her cheek once more
Blushed bright beneath my burning kiss:
I propped her head up as before,
Only, this time my shoulder bore
Her head, which droops upon it still.
The smiling rosy little head,
So glad it has its utmost will,
That all it scorned at once is fled,
And I, its love, am gained instead!
Porphyria's love: she guessed not how
Her darling one wish would be heard.
And thus we sit together now,
And all night long we have not stirred,
And yet God has not said a word!

Robert Browning

Warren Gibbs
died by arsenic poisoning
Mar. 23, 1860
Ae. 36 yrs. 5 mos. 23 d'ys.

Think, my friends, when this you see
How my wife hath dealt by me
She in some oysters did prepare
Some poison for my lot and share
Then of the same I did partake
And Nature yielded to its fate
Before she my wife became
Mary Felton was her name.

Erected by his brother, Wm. Gibbs

Pelham, Massachusetts
Anon.

Crime leaves a trail like a water-beetle;
Like a snail, it leaves its shine;
Like a horse-mango it leaves its reek.

Malay proverb

from UNDER MILK WOOD

FIRST VOICE

Mr Pugh, in the School House opposite, takes up the morning tea to Mrs Pugh, and whispers on the stairs

MR PUGH

Here's your arsenic, dear.
And your weedkiller biscuit.
I've throttled your parakeet.
I've spat in the vases.
I've put cheese in the mouseholes.
Here's your . . .
. . . nice tea, dear.

MRS PUGH

Too much sugar.

MR PUGH

You haven't tasted it yet, dear.

MRS PUGH

Too much milk, then.

Dylan Thomas

— THE DORKING THIGH —

About to marry and invest
Their lives in safety and routine
Stanley and June required a nest
And came down on the 4.15.

The agent drove them to the Posh Estate
And showed them several habitations.
None did. The afternoon got late
With questions, doubts, and explanations.

Then day grew dim and Stan fatigued
And disappointment raised its head,
But June declared herself intrigued
To know where that last turning led.

It led to a Tudor snuggery styled
'Ye Kumfi Nooklet' on the gate.
'A gem of a home,' the salesman smiled,
'My pet place on the whole estate;

'It's not quite finished, but you'll see
Good taste itself.' They went inside.
'This little place is built to be
A husband's joy, a housewife's pride.'

They saw the white convenient sink,
The modernistic chimneypiece,
June gasped for joy, Stan gave a wink
To say, 'Well, here our quest can cease.'

The salesman purred (he'd managed well)
And June undid a cupboard door.
'For linen,' she beamed. And out there fell
A nameless Something on the floor.

'Something the workmen left, I expect,'
The agent said, as it fell at his feet,
Nor knew that his chance of a sale was wrecked.
'Good heavens, it must be a joint of meat!'

Ah yes, it was meat, it was meat all right,
A joint those three will never forget –
For they stood alone in the Surrey night
With the severed thigh of a plump brunette . . .

* * *

Early and late, early and late,
Traffic was jammed round the Posh Estate,
And the papers were full of the Dorking Thigh
And who, and when, and where, and why.

A trouser button was found in the mud.
(Who made it? Who wore it? Who lost it? Who knows?)
But no one found a trace of blood
Or her body or face, or the spoiler of those.

He's acting a play in the common air
On which no curtain can ever come down.
Though 'Ye Kumfi Nooklet' was shifted elsewhere
June made Stan take a flat in town.

William Plomer

— LATE LAST NIGHT ... —

Late last night I slew my wife,
Stretched her on the parquet flooring,
I was loath to take her life,
But I had to stop her snoring.

Harry Graham

DAVY CROCKETT

Born on a table-top in Joe's café
dirtiest place in the USA
polished off his father when he was only three
polished off his mother with DDT
Davy Davy Crockett
King of the wild frontier

Anon.

Lizzie Borden took an axe,
Gave her father forty whacks,
When she saw what she had done
She gave her mother forty-one.

Anon.

BAG-SNATCHING IN DUBLIN

Sisley
Walked so nicely
With footsteps so discreet
To see her pass
You'd never guess
She walked upon the street.
Down where the Liffy waters' turgid flood
Churns up to greet the ocean-driven mud.
A bruiser in a fix
Murdered her for 6/6.

Stevie Smith

A CASE OF MURDER

They should not have left him there alone,
Alone that is except for the cat.
He was only nine, not old enough
To be left alone in a basement flat,
Alone, that is, except for the cat.
A dog would have been a different thing,
A big gruff dog with slashing jaws,
But a cat with round eyes mad as gold,
Plump as a cushion with tucked-in paws –
Better have left him with a fair-sized rat!
But what they did was leave him with a cat.
He hated that cat; he watched it sit,
A buzzing machine of soft black stuff,
He sat and watched and he hated it,
Snug in its fur, hot blood in a muff,
And its mad gold stare and the way it sat
Crooning dark warmth: he loathed all that.
So he took Daddy's stick and he hit the cat.
Then quick as a sudden crack in glass
It hissed, black flash, to a hiding place
In the dust and dark beneath the couch,
And he followed the grin on his new-made face,
A wide-eyed, frightened snarl of a grin,
And he took the stick and he thrust it in,
Hard and quick in the furry dark,
The black fur squealed and he felt his skin
Prickle with sparks of dry delight.

Then the cat again came into sight,
Shot for the door that wasn't quite shut,
But the boy, quick too, slammed fast the door:
The cat, half-through, was cracked like a nut
And the soft black thud was dumped on the floor.
Then the boy was suddenly terrified
And he bit his knuckles and cried and cried;
But he had to do something with the dead thing there.
His eyes squeezed beads of salty prayer
But the wound of fear gaped wide and raw;
He dared not touch the thing with his hands
So he fetched a spade and shovelled it
And dumped the load of heavy fur
In the spidery cupboard under the stair
Where it's been for years, and though it died
It's grown in that cupboard and its hot low purr
Grows slowly louder year by year:
There'll not be a corner for the boy to hide
When the cupboard swells and all sides split
And the huge black cat pads out of it.

Vernon Scannell

AN EMPTY PHONE BOX

Coolly, girl, you climbed to the winter uplands,
To the moors where hedges yield their place to wire,
Changing down a gear as the roadway mounted,
A track through moorland, lit by slanting fire.

The sun invents its journey down to darkness,
The Brennig lakes like knives transmit their gleam.
Behind you Pentrefoelas, Denbigh ahead.
You switch on music to soothe your self-esteem.

Suddenly a cut-out. The motor stops its beat.
You open the bonnet, the engine shows its heart.
With frozen fingers you release the two spring clips
And hold the distributor in your glove apart.

Now you can see the tiny spring is broken.
Nothing to do except to ring the AA.
Your brain goes spinning, plotting your position,
Remembering a phone box, half a mile away.

The road glides on, a snake along a drain,
A culvert in which ice constricts and bites
Deep into every footstep's wound,
Until you reach the phone box's snow-draped lights.

Glass versus snow, and snug to your hand the phone.
You raise it. It breathes. It is alive. The valve
Opens to let you get your finger in.
You dial. The clicks relax you like a salve.

A Renault cruises by you all unknown.
It stops. A gentleman stands by your side.
And then goes out. No clue except the floor,
The bloodstained slush, to witness how you died.

Edward Lloyd

Based on an incident that took place on a mountain road outside Denbigh, north Wales, in the early 1980s

HER SECOND HUSBAND HEARS HER STORY

'Still, Dear, it is incredible to me
        That here, alone,
You should have sewed him up until he died,
And in this very bed. I do not see
How you could do it, seeing what might betide.'

'Well, he came home one midnight, liquored deep –
        Worse than I'd known –
And lay down heavily, and soundly slept:
Then, desperate driven, I thought of it, to keep
Him from me when he woke. Being an adept

'With needle and thimble, as he snored, click-click
        An hour I'd sewn,
Till, had he roused, he couldn't have moved from bed,
So tightly laced in sheet and quilt and tick
He lay. And in the morning he was dead.

'Ere people came I drew the stitches out,
        And thus 'twas shown
To be a stroke.' – 'It's a strange tale!' said he.
'And this same bed?' – 'Yes, here it came about.
'Well, it sounds strange – told here and now to me.

'Did you intend his death by your tight lacing?'
        'O, that I cannot own.
I could not think of else that would avail
When he should wake up, and attempt embracing.' –
        'Well, it's a cool queer tale!'

Thomas Hardy

MURDER!

I can recall that distant valley,
the years-old rotting bridge,
the woman on the bay mare flying over
in a dark cloud of dust, pale-cheeked and graceless,
'Murder!'
She screamed it out.
I cannot lose this memory anywhere,
how people ran behind her
dropping their sickles down into the grass.
And sad and strange he was lying
over the far side of a small hill,
with an imperceptible wound under the rib,
being innocently murdered for money . . .
I recollect the darkness of the mud,
hear the hooves,
I dream the woman in her cloud of dust.
'Murder!'
tearing my heart open.

I find it hard to live in the world,
hearing that scream, hard:
I am not yet used to human death.
I have sometimes seen, deplore it as you wish,
a spirit's imperceptible destruction.
Watching a senior comrade at his business
it terrifies me to divine his death
hardening over his face and his features.
I am not strong enough,
clench my teeth, stay silent.
'Murder!'
I all but scream it out.

Yevgeny Yevtushenko

— ONE QUESTION FROM A BULLET —

I want to give up being a bullet
I've been a bullet too long

I want to be an innocent coin
in the hand of a child
and be squeezed through the slot
of a bubblegum machine

I want to give up being a bullet
I've been a bullet too long

I want to be a good luck seed
lying idle in somebody's pocket
or some ordinary little stone
on the way to becoming an earring
or just lying there unknown
among a crowd of other ordinary stones

I want to give up being a bullet
I've been a bullet too long

The question is
Can you give up being a killer?

John Agard

On the Scent

'Brilliant Police Investigation' . . . The remarkable acumen by which Inspector McKinnon deduced from the smell of paint that some other smell, that of gas, for example, might be concealed; the bold deduction that the strong-room might also be the death-chamber; and the subsequent inquiry which led to the discovery of the bodies in a disused well, cleverly concealed by a dog-kennel, should live in the history of crime as a standing example of the intelligence of our professional detectives . . .

from The Case-Book of Sherlock Holmes,
Sir Arthur Conan Doyle (1859–1930)

– DR WATSON'S LAMENT –

'We are called to solve a case
In one of England's Stately Homes.
I am simply Dr Watson,
You're the famous Sherlock Holmes.
You walk on intently listening,
I remain two steps behind.
Brilliantly your mind deduces
Theories of every kind;
Earning international praises,
Everywhere your fancy roams.'

'Elementary, my dear Watson.'
'Quite amazing, my dear Holmes.'

'I'm sent first to do the spadework,
Sherlock Holmes will follow on.
I'm to scatter crumbs of comfort,
Bringing all his benison.
I placate the landed gentry,
Keep the local police force sweet;
You arrive in deep disguises,
Foiling me when next we meet,
Make me seem a bumbling clodpole
With your coalmen and your crones.'

'Merely child's play, my dear Watson.'
'If you say so, my dear Holmes.'

'Summoned into lukewarm breakfast,
Munching leathery toast, while you
Madly scrape your wretched fiddle,
Interview a prince or two;
Send me on a minor errand,
And returning, out of breath,
Find you ailing.' 'Leave me, Watson,
I am feeling sick to death.'
('Drugged up to the eyeballs rather,
Uttering pathetic moans.')

'I'll call you when I want you, Watson.'
'Go to blazes, my dear Holmes.'

David King

THE POLICEMAN'S LOT

When a felon's not engaged in his employment
  Or maturing his felonious little plans,
His capacity for innocent enjoyment
  Is just as great as any honest man's.
Our feelings we with difficulty smother
  When constabulary duty's to be done:
Ah, take one consideration with another,
  A policeman's lot is not a happy one!

When the enterprising burglar isn't burgling,
  When the cut-throat isn't occupied in crime,
He loves to hear the little brook a-gurgling,
  And listen to the merry village chime.
When the coster's finished jumping on his mother,
  He loves to lie a-basking in the sun:
Ah, take one consideration with another,
  The policeman's lot is not a happy one!

W. S. Gilbert

THE ARREST OF OSCAR WILDE AT THE CADOGAN HOTEL

He sipped at a weak hock and seltzer
   As he gazed at the London skies
Through the Nottingham lace of the curtains
   Or was it his bees-winged eyes?

To the right and before him Pont Street
   Did tower in her new built red,
As hard as the morning gaslight
   That shone on his unmade bed,

'I want some more hock in my seltzer,
   And Robbie, please give me your hand –
Is this the end or beginning?
   How can I understand?

'So you've brought me the latest *Yellow Book*:
   And Buchan has got in it now:
Approval of what is approved of
   Is as false as a well-kept vow.

'More hock, Robbie – where is the seltzer?
   Dear boy, pull again at the bell!
They are all little better than *cretins*,
   Though this *is* the Cadogan Hotel.

'One astrakhan coat is at Willis's –
   Another one's at the Savoy:
Do fetch my morocco portmanteau,
   And bring them on later, dear boy.'

A thump and a murmur of voices –
   ('Oh why must they make such a din?')
As the door of the bedroom swung open
   And TWO PLAIN CLOTHES POLICEMEN came in:

'Mr Woilde, we 'ave come for tew take yew
   Where felons and criminals dwell:
We must ask yew tew leave with us quoietly
   For this *is* the Cadogan Hotel.'

He rose, and he put down *The Yellow Book.*
   He staggered – and, terrible-eyed,
He brushed past the palms on the staircase
   And was helped to a hansom outside.

John Betjeman

In 1895 the writer, Oscar Wilde, was arrested for homosexual practices. The Yellow Book *published fashionable artists and writers of the time.*

UNCLE ALBERT

When I was almost eight years old
My Uncle Albert came to stay;
He wore a watch-chain made of gold
And sometimes he would let me play
With both the chain and gleaming watch,
And though at times I might be rough
He never seemed to bother much.
He smelled of shaving soap and snuff,
To me he was a kind of God,
Immensely wise and strong and kind,
And so I thought it rather odd
When I came home from school to find
Two strangers, menacing and tall,
In the parlour, looking grim
As Albert – suddenly quite small –
Let them rudely hustle him
Out to where a black car stood.
Both Albert and his watch and chain
Disappeared that day for good.
My parents said he'd gone to Spain.

Vernon Scannell

IN-A BRIXTAN MARKIT

I walk in-a Brixtan markit,
believin I a respectable man,
you know. An wha happn?

Policeman come straight up
an search mi bag!
Man – straight to mi.
Like them did a-wait fi mi.
Come search mi bag, man.

Fi mi bag!
An wha them si in deh?
Two piece a yam, a dasheen,
a han a banana, a piece a pork
an mi lates Bob Marley.

Man all a suddn I feel
mi head nah fi mi. This yah now
is when man kill somody, nah!

'Tony', I sey, 'hol on. Hol on,
Tony. Dohn shove. Dohn shove.
Dohn move neidda fis, tongue
nor emotion. Battn down, Tony.
Battn down.' An, man, Tony win.

James Berry

BROOKLYN COP

Built like a gorilla but less timid,
thick-fleshed, steak-coloured, with two
hieroglyphs in his face that mean
trouble, he walks the sidewalk and the
thin tissue over violence. This morning
when he said, 'See you, babe' to his wife,
he hoped it, he truly hoped it.
He is a gorilla
to whom 'Hiya, honey' is no cliché.

Should the tissue tear, should he plunge through
into violence, what clubbings, what
gunshots between Phoebe's
Whamburger and Louie's Place.

Who would be him, gorilla with a nightstick,
whose home is a place
he might, this time, never get back to?

And who would be who have to be
his victims?

Norman MacCaig

A POLICE STATION DITTY

Then it's collar 'im tight,
  In the name of the Law!
'Ustle 'im, shake 'im till 'e's sick!
  Wot, 'e *would*, would 'e? Well,
  Then yer've got ter give 'im 'Ell,
An' it's trunch, trunch, truncheon does the trick!

Max Beerbohm

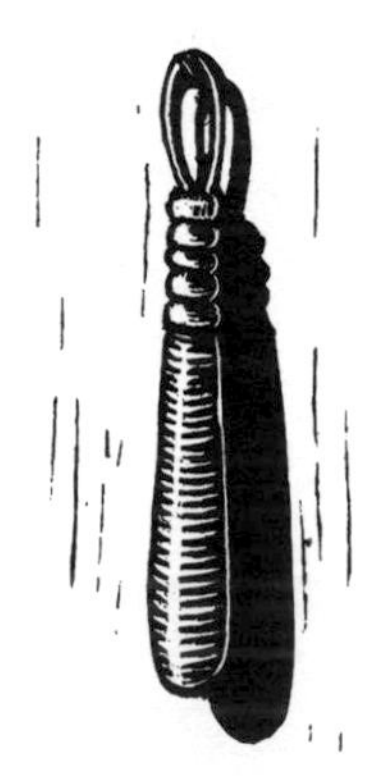

YES, OFFICER

It was about the time of day you mention, yes.
I remember noticing the quality of light
beyond the bridge. I lit a cigarette.

I saw some birds. I knew the words for them
and their collective noun. A skein of geese. This cell
is further away from anywhere I've ever been. Perhaps.

I was in love. *For God's sake, don't.*
Fear is the first taste of blood in a dry mouth.
I have no alibi. Yes, I used to have a beard.

No, no. I wouldn't use that phrase. The more you ask
the less I have to say. There was a woman crying
on the towpath, dressed in grey. *Please.* Sir.

Without my own language, I am a blind man
in the wrong house. Here come the fists, the boots.
I curl in a corner, uttering empty vowels until

they have their truth. That is my full name.
With my good arm I sign a forgery. Yes, Officer,
I did. I did and these, your words, admit it.

Carol Ann Duffy

- WHO BUT THE LORD? -

I looked and I saw
That man they call the Law.
He was coming
Down the street at me!
I had visions in my head
Of being laid out cold and dead,
Or else murdered
By the third degree.

I said, *O, Lord, if you can,*
Save me from that man!
Don't let him make a pulp out of me!
But the Lord he was not quick.
The Law raised up his stick
And beat the living hell
Out of me!

Now, I do not understand
Why God don't protect a man
From police brutality.
Being poor and black,
I've no weapon to strike back
So who but the Lord
Can protect me?

Langston Hughes

'No,' said Charles Peace,
'I can't 'ardly blame the perlice.
They 'as their faults, it is true,
But I sees their point of view.'

E. C. Bentley

Charles Peace, the most successful burglar of Victorian times, shot a policeman, confessing in time to save an innocent man from the gallows. Before he was hanged, he sent his wife a card saying: 'In Memory of Charles Peace who was executed in Armley Prison, Tuesday February 25th 1879. Aged 47. For that I done but never intended.'

THE SUSPECT

Asked me for a match suddenly / with his hand up
I thought he was after my wallet
gave him a shove / he fell down
dead on the pavement at my feet
he was forty-two, a respectable man they said
anyone can have a bad heart I told the police
but they've held me five hours and don't
tell me the innocent don't feel
guilty in the glaring chair

I didn't kill you / I didn't know you
I did push you / I did fear you
accusing me from the mortuary drawer
like a damned white ghost I don't believe in
– then why were you afraid / are you used to attacks
by men who want a match / what sort
of life you lead / you were bloody quick
with your hands when you pushed him
what did you think he was and do you think
we don't know what you are / take it
all down / the sweat of the innocent by god we'll see
and not by the hundred-watt bulb of the anglepoise either
give him a clip on the ear jack / you
bastard in your shroud if I feared you then
I hate you now you
no I don't you poor dead man I put you there
I don't I don't
but just

if you could get up / to speak for me
I am on trial / do you understand
I am not guilty / whatever the light says
whatever the sweat says
/ they've noticed my old scar
to be killed by a dead man is no fight
they're starting again
so / your story is he asked you for a light
– yes suddenly / and put his hand up / I thought
he was after my wallet, gave him
a shove, he fell as I told you
dead, it was his heart,
at my feet, as I said

Edwin Morgan

SEND FOR LORD TIMOTHY

The Squire is in his library. He is rather worried.
Lady Constance has been found stabbed in the locked Blue Room, clutching in her hand
A fragment of an Egyptian papyrus. His degenerate half-brother
Is on his way back from New South Wales.
And what was the butler, Glubb,
Doing in the neolithic stone-circle
Up there on the hill, known to the local rustics
From time immemorial as the Nine Lillywhite Boys?
The Vicar is curiously learned
In Renaissance toxicology. A greenish Hottentot,
Armed with a knobkerrie, is concealed in the laurel bushes.

Mother Mary Tiresias is in her parlour.
She is rather worried. Sister Mary Josephus
Has been found suffocated in the scriptorium,
Clutching in her hand a somewhat unspeakable
Central American fetish. Why was the little novice,
Sister Agnes, suddenly struck speechless
Walking in the herbarium? The chaplain, Fr O'Goose,
Is almost too profoundly read
In the darker aspects of fourth-century neo-Platonism.
An Eskimo, armed with a harpoon
Is lurking in the organ loft.

The Warden of St Phenol's is in his study.
He is rather worried. Professor Ostracoderm
Has been found strangled on one of the Gothic turrets,
Clutching in his hand a patchouli-scented
Lady's chiffon handkerchief.
The brilliant undergraduate they unjustly sent down
Has transmitted an obscure message in Greek elegiacs
All the way from Tashkent. Whom was the Domestic Bursar
Planning to meet in that evil-smelling
Riverside tavern? Why was the Senior Fellow,
Old Doctor Mousebracket, locked in among the incunabula?
An aboriginal Filipino pygmy,
Armed with a blow-pipe and poisoned darts, is hiding behind
The statue of Pallas Athene.

A dark cloud of suspicion broods over all. But even now
Lord Timothy Pratincole (the chinless wonder
With a brain like Leonardo's) or Chief Inspector Palefox
(Although a policeman, patently a gentleman,
And with a First in Greats) or that eccentric scholar,
Monsignor Monstrance, alights from the chuffing train,
Has booked a room at the local hostelry
(*The Dragon of Wantley*) and is chatting up Mine Host,
Entirely democratically, noting down
Local rumours and folk-lore.

Now read on. The murderer will be unmasked,
The cloud of guilt dispersed, the church clock stuck at three,
And the year always
Nineteen twenty or thirty something,
Honey for tea, and nothing
Will ever really happen again.

John Heath-Stubbs

SECURITY

I shot him
because he fired at me.

I shot him
because he was pointing a gun at me.

I shot him
because he went for his gun.

I shot him
because he made a hand movement.

I shot him
as he lay on the ground
because these bastards
are at their most dangerous

when they're
          perfectly
                    still.

Michael Levene

THE VILLAGE CONSTABLE

Ah! what a moighty wicked place our village it'd be
If it wasn't vur the care Oi takes of crime ter keep it free,
Oi've taught 'un ter respect the law since Oi've been in the force,
An' wot Oi sez they 'as ter do, they 'as ter do, of course.
Oi can't 'ave that, Oi sez, Oi can't, Oi bain't agoin' ter tell 'ee why,
An' don' 'ee try no tricks on cos Oi'm mighty sharp an' floy –
Oi can't 'ave that, Oi sez, Oi can't, an' you may stand an' give Oi jaw,
But when Oi sez a thing, Oi sez, the thing I sez be law.

It's 'ard work, though, vor Muddleton's a moighty busy place,
There's foive an' forty people an' they loikes ter go the pace.
But Lor! Oi've got un all inside the 'oller of my 'and,
They dursent call their souls their own, Oi tell thee 'as it's grand.
Oi can't 'ave that, Oi sez, Oi can't, Oi bain't agoin' ter tell 'ee why,
An' don' 'ee try no tricks on cos Oi'm mighty sharp an' floy –
Oi can't 'ave that, Oi sez, Oi can't. Ah! you may stand an' give Oi jaw,
But when Oi sez a thing, Oi sez, the thing Oi sez be law.

Albert Chevalier and Alfred H. West

— SERGEANT BROWN'S PARROT —

Many policemen wear upon their shoulders
Cunning little radios. To pass away the time
They talk about the traffic to them, listen to the news,
And it helps them to Keep Down Crime.

But Sergeant Brown, he wears upon his shoulder
A tall green parrot as he's walking up and down
And all the parrot says is 'Who's-a-pretty-boy-then?'
'I am,' says Sergeant Brown.

Kit Wright

On Trial

Laws are like spider's-webs, which, if anything small falls into them, they ensnare it, but large things break through and escape.

7th–6th century BC

IDENTITY PARADE

No he wasn't very *tall*
And, no he wasn't very *short*
He was what you'd really call
A fairly *ordinary* sort.

No, his hair it wasn't *dark*
But then you'd hardly call it *fair*;
Not a color you'd remark,
Just like – well, you know, like *hair*!

Yes his suit was sort of *brown*
Though you could have called it *gray*.
Were his cuffs turned up or down?
Now that I'd hardly like to say.

He was not exactly *fat*
But then I wouldn't call him *thin*.
I don't *think* his feet were flat.
His toes turned *out*. Or was it *in*!

His tie was vivid green,
Or, half a minute, was it blue?
Well you know just what I mean:
It was quite a brilliant hue.

His face was somewhat red,
        Or let me think now, was it pale?
He had a heavy lightsome tread.
        Oh, yes, I'm sure that he was male!

Would I know the man again?
        Do you take me for a dunce?
Out of twenty thousand men
        I'd recognize *that* man at once.

Anon.

PRISONER AND JUDGE

1

The prisoner was walking round and round the prison yard.
He had a low forehead and cruel eyes;
You couldn't trust him anywhere.

He dressed up as a judge; he put on a wig and robes
And sat in court in the judge's place.
And everyone said:
'What a deep forehead he has, what learned eyes!
How wise he looks!
You could trust him anywhere.'

2

The judge was sitting in court in the judge's place.
He had a deep forehead and learned eyes;
You could trust him anywhere.

He dressed up as a prisoner; he put on prisoner's clothes
And walked round and round the prison yard.
And everyone said:
'What a low forehead he has, what cruel eyes!
How stupid he looks!
You couldn't trust him anywhere.'

Ian Serraillier

THE JUDGE'S MONOLOGUE

after signing his first death sentence

This my hand that once wrote letters of love,
today has written the sentence of death for a wretch
to be hanged by the neck till he is dead.

He was a lover – this youth I sentenced to death –
who had killed his sweetheart, strangling her with her hair

twisted ropewise. Why? In a fit of what?
He wouldn't answer. Yet didn't break down,
being touched, it seemed, beyond the breaking point.

Firm in his confession, he left me no escape
from signing his death-warrant.
And flat on him fell the grim prospect
of choking to death, dangling from the end of a rope.

He is at rest, this wretch I doomed to death,
thinking 'I deserve it and justice has been done.'
But oh, how his face will haunt my restless soul
after he is hanged by the neck until he is dead!

Pranab Bandyopadhyay
(translated from the Bengali by Ajit Krishna Basu)

CORONER'S JURY

He was the doctor up to Combe,
Quiet-spoke, dark, weared a moustache,
And one night his wife's mother died
After her meal, and he was tried
For poisoning her.

Evidence come up dark's a bag,
But onions is like arsenic:
'Twas eating they, his lawyer said,
And rabbit, 'fore she went to bed,
That took her off.

Jury withdrew. 'He saved my child,'
Says 'Lias Lee. 'Think to his wife,'
Says one. 'I tell 'ee, a nit's life
That there old 'ooman led 'em both –
Tedious old toad.'

'Give en six months,' says easy Joe.
'You can't do that, sirs,' foreman said,
''Tis neck or nothing, yes or no.'
'All right then, sir,' says Joe. ''Tis no,
Not guilty, sir.'

'You, Jabez Halls?' 'I brings it in
Rabbit and onions; that's my thought.
If that didn' kill her, sirs, it ought,
To her age.' So us brought it in
Rabbit and onions.

Doctor went free, but missis died
Soon afterward, she broke her heart.
Still Doctor bide on twenty year
Walking thc moors, keeping apart
And quiet, like.

L. A. G. Strong

Report in *The Guardian*:

Man sentenced in Paris to eight years in prison for killing his second wife after she had served him an overdone roast. Judge stated that he was being lenient as he felt sympathy with the accused as cooking was an essential virtue in a wife. The prisoner had also killed his first wife for serving underdone meat.

Boil the judge slowly
till done to a turn
good cooking is paramount in life.
Flavour him sweetly
do not let him burn
show yourself a virtuous wife.
Serve him up proudly
as befits a fine meal,
carve him up swiftly
before juices congeal
relish each morsel
so he can truly reveal
good cooking is more important than life.

Peggy Poole

THE SURPRISING SONG OF THE KING'S COUNSEL

Now, Mrs Green, attend to me,
For I'm Sir Buster Blow, KC.
  The question what
  Is true or not
    Is highly complicated,
And while I would not say that you
Have stated that which is not true,
  It is my case
  That what took place
    Was not as you have stated.
Not that it matters, Ma'am, a lot
If what you've said was true or not,
  For I've a knack
  Of making black
    Resemble white or yellow,
And in ten minutes, Ma'am, or less,
The Judge, the Jury and the Press
  Will all decide
  That you have lied
    And I'm a clever fellow!

Blow! Blow! Sir Buster Blow!
Sir Buster Blow's a-blowing!

Nor hope with nimble repartee
To get the better, Ma'am, of me;
    No woman yet
    Contrived to get
        Away with that, young lady!
Though I may call you any name
Don't think that you can do the same,
    For I'm afraid
    You are not paid
        To show that I am shady.
But I have been retained to blast
Your future and expose your past,
    A process which
    Will make you itch
        But move the Court to chuckles!
And if you falter, blush or blink,
The Jury will know what to think,
    While if you try
    A smart reply,
        The Judge will rap your knuckles.

    Blow! Blow! Sir Buster Blow!
        Sir Buster Blow's a-blowing!

Now take your mind back, Mrs Green.
Where were you, please, at 8.15
  On Saturday
  The 6th of May?
    And were you wearing knickers?
And did you, Mrs Green, or not
Spend Easter Monday in a yacht?
  And do you swear
  The persons there
    Consumed teetotal liquors?
Would it be Friday then, or June?
Who else went up in the balloon?
  Why did he fall?
  You can't recall?
    Well, that will suit me nicely.
You knew Lord Lavender, I think,
Who died not long ago of drink?
  You've never read
  A book in bed?
    I thought as much. Precisely!

Blow! Blow! Sir Buster Blow!
  Sir Buster Blow's a-blowing!

Now at the age of one or two
Were you discovered at the Zoo,
  Abandoned in
  A biscuit-tin
    By your ungrateful mother?
At any rate – I see you wince –
You have not seen your parents since,
  But after that
  Were nourished at
    Some nunnery or other?
Have you a mole behind the ear?
Do you prefer thick soup to clear?
  And when you dine
  Do you take wine,
    Dear Mrs Green, or water?
I thought as much! I knew the face.
My Lord, I must conclude the case –
  Embrace me, dear!
  My Lord, it's clear
    The witness is my daughter!

  Blow! Blow! Sir Buster Blow!
    Sir Buster Blow's a-blowing!

A. P. Herbert

THE INQUEST

I took my oath I would inquire,
  Without affection, hate, or wrath,
Into the death of Ada Wright –
  So help me God! I took that oath.

When I went out to see the corpse,
  The four months' babe that died so young,
I judged it was seven pounds in weight,
  And little more than one foot long.

One eye, that had a yellow lid,
  Was shut – so was the mouth, that smiled;
The left eye open, shining bright –
  It seemed a knowing little child.

For as I looked at that one eye,
  It seemed to laugh, and say with glee:
'What caused my death you'll never know –
  Perhaps my mother murdered me.'

When I went into court again,
  To hear the mother's evidence –
It was a love-child, she explained.
  And smiled, for our intelligence.

'Now, Gentlemen of the Jury,' said
  The coroner – 'this woman's child
By misadventure met its death.'
  'Aye, aye,' said we. The mother smiled.

And I could see that child's one eye
  Which seemed to laugh, and say with glee:
'What caused my death you'll never know –
  Perhaps my mother murdered me.'

W. H. Davies

from GOING ON

Just hypothermia (Coroner
for St Pancras announces)
caused this particular death.
5-year-old Elliot Hinds'

mum and her boyfriend were said to have
got the idea from watching
some late-night film on TV.
Anyway, Elliot died.

What he had done was to wet the bed
(that most heinous of child crimes)
so, his mum's boyfriend took charge –
held the boy under a shower

(full on the 'Cold' setting) for about
15 minutes. It seems that
'Elliot usually screamed
while being given cold showers'.

Sagely, the Coroner's jury re-
turns the old 'Misadventure'.
'Ankle, I have little doubt,
not through vindictiveness, but

probably just out of some way of
trying to discipline this lad,
latched on to this form of cure.'
(¼ hour's icy-cold shower.)

So, the Director of Public
Prosecutions decides that
  there is *not* gross negligence;
  therefore no Manslaughter charge.

Peter Reading

— THE JUSTICE OF THE PEACE —

Distinguish carefully between these two,
  This thing is yours, that other thing is mine.
You have a shirt, a brimless hat, a shoe
  And half a coat. I am the Lord benign
Of fifty hundred acres of fat land
To which I have a right. You understand?

I have a right because I have, because,
  Because I have – because I have a right.
Now be quite calm and good, obey the laws,
  Remember your low station, do not fight
Against the goad, because, you know, it pricks
Whenever the uncleanly demos kicks.

I do not envy you your hat, your shoe.
  Why should you envy me my small estate?
It's fearfully illogical in you
  To fight with economic force and fate.
Moreover, I have got the upper hand,
And mean to keep it. Do you understand?

Hilaire Belloc

THE CIRCUIT JUDGE

Take note, passers-by, of the sharp erosions
Eaten in my head-stone by the wind and rain –
Almost as if an intangible Nemesis or hatred
Were marking scores against me,
But to destroy, and not preserve, my memory.
I in life was the Circuit Judge, a maker of notches,
Deciding cases on the points the lawyers scored,
Not on the right of the matter.
O wind and rain, leave my head-stone alone!
For worse than the anger of the wronged,
The curses of the poor,
Was to lie speechless, yet with vision clear,
Seeing that even Hod Putt, the murderer,
Hanged by my sentence,
Was innocent in soul compared with me.

Edgar Lee Masters

God works a wonder now and then,
Here, though a lawyer, was an honest man.

Rineton Churchyard, Norfolk

Anon.

from ON TRIAL

8: The Undecided

A face that burrowed a moustache to hide in
sat amongst those who never held strong views;
good people, always eager to confide in
others just how hard it was to choose,
preferring always movement with a crowd;
readers of tabloids tarting up the news
to titilating entertainment, loud
with scandals, murders, rapes and sexual stews.
All of which shook their heads to virtuous *tuts*,
yet proved essential reading for relaxing;
this was for real, a maze of *ifs* and *buts*,
the arguments, bewilderingly taxing;
a flock of fundamentalist Don't Knows,
Guilty, if you all say so, I suppose.

Maurice Lindsay

BALLAD OF THE LONG DROP

We dropped a chap that raped a child:
He gave no trouble, kind and mild.
We dropped a kid that killed a cop:
He made a lightish drop.

We dropped a well-fed man who bled
Old ladies – and the prayers he said!
We dropped a gangster who was bold
But shivered with the cold.

We dropped a gentlemanly rake
Who said it wasn't our mistake
We dropped a fool or two who tried
To struggle as they died.

We dropped a lad who killed by whim,
Who cursed us as we pinioned him.
We dropped a girl who shot a bloke
Because her heart was broke.

Her heart was broke. She did him in
For love: but love like hers is sin.
We dropped her, for we drop them straight
For love as well as hate.

For love as well as hate we serve
To break the neck and break the nerve
Of those who break the laws of man:
We serve you all as best we can.

John Pudney

COMEBACK

The last and retired executioner spends
a day on location advising on a hanging scene
in a film. At the end of it the
director thanks him. He replies:
'Thank you *... it's been a long time.'*

When a hangman hangs up his noose
And retires from the game,
He can think he's of little use,
A forgotten name,
A hasbeen deathshead, a snuffed-
Out old hellflame,

A superannuated
Extinction bore,
Lonely and dumb and dated,
Shoved out the door
By new and pacific fashions,
A dinosaur.

When the executioner bites
The dust of old age,
He sees himself, by his lights,
A turned-over page
Of history that discards
A Killing sage.

But when a movie unreels
In someone's brain
And they ask him his know-how he feels
His oats again!
Back on the tried old track
Of the State-slain.

Back with the dear old Sentence –
He knows the tropes!
Back with the priest's attendance –
Best of Soaps!
Back with the expertise –
He knows the ropes!

So when a hangman returns
And hangs up his hat
Near where his warm fire burns,
He's the better for that –
Keeping his horrible hand in,
And hearing the chat.

Kit Wright

from LAW LIKE LOVE

Law, say the gardeners, is the sun,
Law is the one
All gardeners obey
Tomorrow, yesterday, today.

Law is the wisdom of the old,
The impotent grandfathers feebly scold;
The grandchildren put out a treble tongue,
Law is the senses of the young.

Law, says the priest with a priestly look,
Expounding to an unpriestly people,
Law is the words in my priestly book,
Law is my pulpit and my steeple.

Law, says the judge as he looks down his nose,
Speaking clearly and most severely,
Law is as I've told you before,
Law is as you know I suppose,
Law is but let me explain it once more,
Law is The Law.

Yet law-abiding scholars write:
Law is neither wrong nor right,
Law is only crimes
Punished by places and by times,
Law is the clothes men wear
Anytime, anywhere,
Law is Good morning and Good night.

Others say, Law is our Fate;
Others say, Law is our State;
Others say, others say
Law is no more,
Law has gone away.

And always the loud angry crowd,
Very angry and very loud,
Law is We,
And always the soft idiot softly Me.

W. H. Auden

Doing Time

A prison is a house of care, a place where none can thrive;
A touchstone true to try a friend, a grave for one alive.
Sometimes a place of right, sometimes a place of wrong,
Sometimes a place of rogues and thieves and honest men among.

Inscription on Edinburgh's
Old Tolbooth Prison, Demolished in 1817

— *from* THE BALLAD OF — READING GAOL

There is no chapel on the day
  On which they hang a man:
The Chaplain's heart is far too sick,
  Or his face is far too wan,
Or there is that written in his eyes
  Which none should look upon.

So they kept us close till nigh on noon,
  And then they rang the bell,
And the warders with their jingling keys
  Opened each listening cell,
And down the iron stair we tramped,
  Each from his separate Hell.

Out into God's sweet air we went,
  But not in wonted way,
For this man's face was white with fear,
  And that man's face was grey,
And I never saw sad men who looked
  So wistfully at the day.

I never saw sad men who looked
  With such a wistful eye
Upon that little tent of blue
  We prisoners called the sky,
And at every happy cloud that passed
  In such strange freedom by.

But there were those amongst us all
Who walked with downcast head,
And knew that, had each got his due,
They should have died instead:
He had but killed a thing that lived,
Whilst they had killed the dead.

For he who sins a second time
Wakes a dead soul to pain,
And draws it from its spotted shroud,
And makes it bleed again,
And makes it bleed great gouts of blood,
And makes it bleed in vain!

In Reading gaol by Reading town
There is a pit of shame,
And in it lies a wretched man
Eaten by teeth of flame,
In a burning winding-sheet he lies,
And his grave has got no name.

And there, till Christ call forth the dead,
In silence let him lie:
No need to waste the foolish tear,
Or heave the windy sigh:
The man had killed the thing he loved,
And so he had to die.

And all men kill the thing they love,
By all let this be heard,
Some do it with a bitter look,
Some with a flattering word,
The coward does it with a kiss,
The brave man with a sword!

Oscar Wilde

The poet's own experience of imprisonment in Reading Gaol inspired this poem in 1898.

— HARD —

Body kept in shape.
Body to be proud of.
Fit. Hard. Body
in its prime.

Body kept in shape.
Light on its feet.
See it run.
Punishing itself.

Body kept in shape.
Oblivious to cold.
Heat. Light-fingered.
Watch it.

Body kept in shape.
Lithe. Neat. Catch
it. Red-handed.
Punish it.

Body kept in shape.
Body kept in.
Body in its prime.
Doing time.

Bernard Young

—— BABY DIES —— IN CUPBOARD

(*Independent*, 12 June 1990)

Funny how things turn out.
I'd often had to punish him
worse than that –
when he'd shit himself
or cry for no reason –
and he'd yelled and choked,
frightened me once or twice.

That night I'd had one or two
and he kept carrying on.
I need my sleep; it got to me
his mother stopping out
and him keep calling.
I hit him, shook him.
'Bitch' I kept saying, 'bitch.'

Funny thing is
he didn't make much fuss
didn't seem to mind the dark.
Before I dropped off
I just remember soft weeps
like in his sleep,
like if he'd lost something.

I know he's dead,
I know I shouldn't have
Funny all the same
I'm in here doing time
for when I'm sure he didn't suffer.
But when I really hurt him
no one noticed, no one came.

Carole Satyamurti

PICTURES

O my thirteen pictures are in prison!
O somebody bail them out!
I don't know what they've done, poor things, but justice has arisen
in the shape of half-a-dozen stout
policemen and arrested them, and hauled them off to gaol.
O my nice Boccaccio, how goes your pretty tale
locked up in a dungeon cell
with Eve and the Amazon, the Lizard and the frail
Renascence, all sent to hell
at the whim of six policemen and a magistrate whose stale
sensibilities hate everything that's well.

D. H. Lawrence

On 5 July 1929, thirteen paintings by Lawrence, considered to be obscene, were removed from a London gallery by six policemen.

TO ONE IN PRISON

Today we have remembered sacrifice and glory
And the Cenotaph with flowers is overstocked:
A single gun to soundlessness has clocked
And unified King, Communist, and Tory . . .
I have listened to your broken stumbling story,
And trespassed in your mind, slum-built and shoddy.
You too have shared the Silence; you have knelt
In the cheerless Prison chapel; you have felt
Armistice Day emotion brim your body.

Six years, you say, you've worked at baking bread
(A none-too-wholesome task that must be done
By those whom God appoints). You are twenty-one
(Though I'd have guessed you less). Your father's dead
(Run over by a lorry, I think you said,
In the Great War, while coming home on leave).
Your brother got in trouble and spent three years
In Borstal (all these facts I can believe
Without the reinforcement of your tears).

Your brother failed completely to 'make good';
Your brother died; committed suicide
By turning on the gas, a twelve-month since.
Now you're in prison for stealing what you could:
Mother's in prison for the same offence:
And I've no reason to suspect you lied
When you informed me that you 'only tried
To stick to mother'. I was touched. You stood
So young, so friendless, so remorseful-eyed.

Therefore I find myself compelled to add
A footnote on your candour and humility.
You seem to me a not insensitive lad
Of average emotional ability.
You've 'been upset today'. 'By what?' I query.
'By the two-minute silence.' Then your weeping ...
And then your face, so woebegone and weary.
And now – what use, the pity that I am heaping
Upon your head? What use – to wish you well
And slam the door? Who knows? ... My heart, not yours,
can tell.

Siegfried Sassoon

CONVICTED

I think of him always,
I think of him first thing before light.

Waking,
the warmth of the duvet we might have shared.

I am happy early
until his soft missile homes,
thumps me like frozen snow
thrown by a child.

Then I think
wondering what he thinks
behind bars.

Those brief visits
where I have learned
to make the minutes of our meetings stretch
into infinity.

So long drawn out a curve could comfort
if I didn't keep seeing
his two dark eyes.

His confession must have been rigged.
It took me three months to cry.

Hard times. Christmases
my child hasn't had. She said,
'I don't remember my dad.'

But one bleak Sunday
she found him in the personal box,
in photos, letters, newspaper reports.

She looked at me, my daughter.
Her face came away like old plaster.

My God if I'd sought
self-sacrifice I'd have gone
for a nun.

Although I know in my bones and my blood
he will not come
I think of him late
until my thoughts become

white ash in a cold grate.

Jenny Hamlett

IN THE CAN

Every second is a fishbone that sticks
in the throat. Every hour another slow
Step towards freedom. We're geriatrics
Waiting for release, bribing time to go.
I've give up trying to make anything
Different happen. Mornings: tabloids, page three.
Afternoons: videos or Stephen King,
Answering letters from relatives who bore me.
We're told not to count, but the days mount here
Like thousands of identical stitches
Resentfully sewn into a sampler,
Or a cricket bat made out of matches.
Nights find me scoring walls like a madman,
Totting up runs: one more day in the can.

Rosie Jackson

STRAWBERRIES

Lush, red, frosted white, they sit glistening
in a Tupperware. You slip them to me
Under cover of a whispered story
– Some new scandal – and whilst I'm listening
I bite into the unexpected flesh.
The taste of childhood summer hits my tongue,
That sweet, tart, stolen crop we ate when young.
My eyes close with the pleasure: ripe and fresh.
Two weeks condensed in two hours go quickly:
An officer recalls us, like hired boats
On a pond: 'Time's up!' He rattles keys, gloats
'I've booked you!' 'What for?' His words a sickly
Reminder where we are: *solitary*'s
The fruit for answering back. 'Eating strawberries!'

Rosie Jackson

LAST SUPPERS

Request 1
Pepperoni Pizza, extra anchovies
Hot Fudge Brownie, diet Coke
(Executed)

Request 2
BLT (double order), Dry Martini
Pistachio ice
(No alcohol permitted)
(Executed)

Request 3
Two quarter pounders, fries, relish, side salad
Death by Chocolate, large Pepsi
(Executed)

Request 4
Cucumber Sandwiches (crusts removed)
Strawberries and Clotted cream, pot of Earl Grey
(Thick cream only)
(Executed)

Request 5
T-bone steak, large fries, ketchup
Mama's pumpkin pie
(Mama's pie unavailable)
(Executed)

Request 6
One shiny wormless apple
(Executed)

Request 7
Unleavened bread, water
(Executed)

Request 8
Pastrami on Rye to go
(Unacceptable)
(Executed)

Sue Dymoke

THE BLACK DOG OF NEWDIGATE

(*from Peveril of the Peak*)

'Tis the black ban-dog on our jail.
  Pray look on him,
But at a wary distance; rouse him not –
  He bays not till he worries.

Sir Walter Scott

ON THE EMBANKMENT

Down on the sunlit ebb with the wind in her sails and free
Of cable and anchor she swept rejoicing to seek the sea.

And my eyes and my heart swept out with her,
When at my elbow I felt a stir
And glancing down, I saw a lad –
A shambling lad with shifty air,
Weak-chested, stunted, and ill-clad –
Who watched her with unseeing stare.

Dull watery grey eyes he had,
Blinking beneath the slouching cap
That hid the low-browed, close-cropped head;
And as I turned to him he said,
With hopeless hang-dog air –
Just out of gaol three days ago,
And I'll be back before I know,
For nothing else is left a chap
When once he's been inside ... and so ...
Then dumb he stood with sightless stare
Set on the sunlit windy sail of the far-off boat that, free
Of anchor and cable, still swept on rejoicing to seek the sea.

My heart is a sunlit windy sail:
My heart is a hopeless lad in gaol.

Wilfrid Gibson

ROGUES' GALLERY

The laws of God, the laws of man,
He may keep that will and can;
Not I: let God and man decree
Laws for themselves and not for me;
And if my ways are not as theirs
Let them mind their own affairs.
Their deeds I judge and much condemn,
Yet when did I make laws for them?
Please yourselves, say, and they
Need only look the other way.

A. E. HOUSMAN *(1859–1936)*

SMART-BOY

I am the Lad: the wide-awake, the smart-boy,
The one who knows the ropes and where he's going,
The easy smiler with the easy money.

I was the kid who got no praise or prizes
Who's now the man to get the peachbloom lovelies:
Black Market Boy with my good mixer manner.

I'm your tall talker in the fug of bar-rooms,
Quick at a deal, an old hand on the dog tracks,
Knowing in clubs, stander at Soho corners.

Go-between guy, I'm wiser than to work for
What the world hands me on a shiny salver,
Me the can't-catch-me-dozing razor-sharp-boy

Ready to set my toe to Order's backside:
Big-shot-to-be, big-city up-and-comer:
Quickstepper, racer, ace among you sleepers.

A. S. J. Tessimond

MY NEIGHBOUR MR NORMANTON

My neighbour Mr Normanton
Who lives at ninety-five
'S as typical an Englishman
As anyone alive.

He wears pin-stripes and bowler-hat.
His accent is sublime.
He keeps a British bull-dog
And British Summer Time.

His shoes are always glassy black
(He never wears the brown);
His brolly's rolled slim as a stick
When he goes up to town.

He much prefers a game of darts
To mah-jong or to chess.
He fancies Chelsea for the Cup
And dotes on G. & S.

Roast beef and Yorkshire pudding are
What he most likes to eat.
His drinks are tea and British beer
And sometimes whisky (neat).

Out of a British briar-pipe
He puffs an Empire smoke
While gazing at his roses (red)
Beneath a British oak.

And in his British garden
Upon St George's Day
He hoists a British Union Jack
And shouts, 'Hip, hip, hooray!'

But tell me, Mr Normanton,
That evening after dark,
Who were those foreign gentlemen
You met in Churchill Park?

You spoke a funny language
I couldn't understand;
And wasn't that some microfilm
You'd hidden in your hand?

And then that note I saw you post
Inside a hollow tree!
When I jumped out you turned about
As quick as quick could be.

Why did you use a hearing-aid
While strolling in the park
And talking to that worried-looking
Admiralty clerk?

The day you took the cypher-book
From underneath a stone,
I'm certain, Mr Normanton,
You thought you were alone.

Your powerful transmitter!
The stations that you call!
I love to watch you through the crack
That's in my bedroom wall.

Oh, thank you, Mr Normanton,
For asking me to tea.
It's really all quite riveting
To clever chaps like me.

What? Will I come and work for you?
Now please don't mention pay.
What super luck I left a note
To say I'd run away!

Is that a gun that's in your hand?
And look! A lethal pill!
And that's a real commando-knife?
I say, this is a thrill!

Of course I've never said a word
About the things you do.
Let's keep it all a secret
Between just me and . . .

Charles Causley

MUTE

‘I stabbed that woman
Right into her heart
And slashed her through and through

Across the gold and blueness
Of her vest, her cloak, her hands,
Her baby too –

But then they whistled,
Gripped my arms,
I felt the strain invade my neck,

Was led through halls
Of multitudes
Where none would hear

That I had come to her
A thousand times,
Had begged for recognition,

Warmth, had craved
A wife, a child, a home
Out of the winter rain!

That muteness stung me
To despair, so on this day
I took a knife to her for all to see.

Only I wonder
Why there was no blood.
My cell is warm and dry.'

Lotte Kramer

note: a man was convicted for damaging a painting in an art gallery.

— *from* A MORAL ALPHABET —

J stands for James, who thought it immaterial
To pay his taxes, Local or Imperial.
In vain the Mother wept, the Wife implored,
James only yawned as though a trifle bored.
The Tax Collector called again, but he
Was met with Persiflage and Repartee.
When James was hauled before the learned Judge,
Who lectured him, he loudly whispered, 'Fudge!'
The Judge was startled from his usual calm,
He struck the desk before him with his palm,
And roared in tones to make the boldest quail,
'*J stands for James*, IT ALSO STANDS FOR JAIL.'
And therefore, on a dark and dreadful day,
Policemen came and took him all away.

The fate of James is typical, and shows
How little mercy people can expect
Who will not pay their taxes (saving those
To which they conscientiously object).

Hilaire Belloc

OLGA PULLOFSKI: THE BEAUTIFUL SPY

The scene is a Military Ballroom,
  The gallant and fair are the dancers.
But who's the Brunette, who with eyes black as jet,
  Fascinates all the Guards and the Lancers?

Chorus

Olga Pullofski, the beautiful spy!
The gay Continental rapscallion!
Some say that she's Russian, and some say she's French,
But her accent is Gin & Italian.
Shame on you! shame on you! Oh, fie fie!
Olga Pullofski, you beautiful spy!

No wonder that England's in danger!
  Disguised as the Lady Godiva
She'll sell to some buyer our glorious Empire
  And the Hippodrome too for a fiver!

Chorus

Olga Pullofski, the beautiful spy
Has evil designs upon Malta.
And in Suez that gal means to dam the Canal
And she'll blast all the rocks in Gibraltar!
Shame on you! shame on you! Oh, fie fie!
Olga Pullofski, you beautiful spy!

The secrets of our Tower of London
  She sold to some great foreign power.
'Twas not Anne Boleyn who at midnight was seen
  Walking round in the Old Bloody Tower – it was

Chorus

Olga Pullofski, the beautiful spy!
The Beefeater she bribed with kisses
Would have willingly given her all the Crown jewels
But he'd lent them that night to the Missus.
Shame on you! shame on you! Oh, fie fie!
Olga Pullofski, you beautiful spy!

R. P. Weston and Bert Lee

This music-hall song is a parody on the true life story of the notorious First World War spy Mata Hari, who set the fashion in films and literature for all dark, glamorous, usually foreign, female traitors.

SHAME

I never shall forget my shame
To find my son had forged my name
If he'd had any thought for others
He might at least have forged his mother's.

Harry Graham

THE FORGER

In broad daylight I forge
your seals and signatures;
in my eye I carry dreams of gems and jewels.
I have no care for your threat of imprisonment;
a thin phial of potassium cyanide
concealed in my inner pocket:
I'm a forger.

I'm the son of a Badshah
as I count packs of forged currency,
accept the black price for counterfeit papers:
I'm a forger.

I walk with the crowd
just to pick your pocket
shearing your ration money;
you're the goody guys – all noise
the miserable people on the earth.
I weep for you, my good friends,
I, too, am built of flesh and blood.
When I'm free from the bond of wine,
I, too, laugh, cry and love
like any one of you;
I also kiss the tender cheek of my beloved child,
I don't poison him.

But to you, my friends,
my only identity:
I'm a forger.

Pranab Bandyopadhyay

THE CRIMINAL

One was a female, who had grievous ill
Wrought in revenge, and she enjoy'd it still:
With death before her, and her fate in view,
Unsated vengeance in her bosom grew:
Sullen she was and threat'ning; in her eye
Glared the stern triumph that she dared to die:
But first a being in the world must leave –
'Twas once reproach; 'twas now a short reprieve.
  She was a pauper bound, who early gave
Her mind to vice, and doubly was a slave;
Upbraided, beaten, held by rough control,
Revenge sustain'd, inspired, and fill'd her soul.
She fired a full-stored barn, confess'd the fact,
And laugh'd at law and justified the act:
Our gentle vicar tried his powers in vain,
She answer'd not, or answer'd with disdain;
Th' approaching fate she heard without a sigh,
And neither cared to live nor fear'd to die.

George Crabbe

WIFE WHO SMASHED TELEVISION GETS JAIL

'She came home, my Lord, and smashed-in the television;
Me and the kids were peaceably watching Kojak
When she marched into the living-room and declared
That if I didn't turn off the television immediately
She'd put her boot through the screen;
I didn't turn it off, so instead she turned it off
– I remember the moment exactly because Kojak
After shooting a dame with the same name as my wife
Snarled at the corpse – Goodnight, Queen Maeve –
And then she took off her boots and smashed in the television;
I had to bring the kids round to my mother's place;
We got there just before the finish of Kojak;
(My mother has a fondness for Kojak, my Lord);
When I returned home my wife had deposited
What was left of the television into the dustbin,
Saying – I didn't get married to a television
And I don't see why my kids or anybody else's kids
Should have a television for a father or mother,
We'd be much better off all down in the pub talking
Or playing bar-billiards –
Whereupon she disappeared off back down again to the pub.'
Justice O'Brádaigh said wives who preferred bar-billiards to family television
Were a threat to the family which was the basic unit of society
As indeed the television itself could be said to be a basic unit of the family
And when as in this case wives expressed their preference in forms of violence
Jail was the only place for them. Leave to appeal was refused.

Paul Durcan

A BALLAD OF JOHN SILVER

We were schooner-rigged and rakish, with a long and lissome hull,
And we flew the pretty colours of the cross-bones and the skull;
We'd a big black Jolly Roger flapping grimly at the fore,
And we sailed the Spanish Water in the happy days of yore.

We'd a long brass gun amidships, like a well-conducted ship,
We had each a brace of pistols and a cutlass at the hip;
It's a point which tells against us, and a fact to be deplored,
But we chased the goodly merchant-men and laid their ships aboard.

Then the dead men fouled the scuppers and the wounded filled the chains,
And the paint-work all was spatter-dashed with other people's brains,
She was boarded, she was looted, she was scuttled till she sank.
And the pale survivors left us by the medium of the plank.

O! then it was (while standing by the taffrail on the poop)
We could hear the drowning folk lament the absent chicken-coop;
Then, having washed the blood away, we'd little else to do
Than to dance a quiet hornpipe as the old salts taught us to.

O! the fiddle on the fo'c's'le, and the slapping naked soles,
And the genial 'Down the middle, Jake, and curtsey when she rolls!'
With the silver seas around us and the pale moon overhead,
And the look-out not a-looking and his pipe-bowl glowing red.

Ah! the pig-tailed, quidding pirates and the pretty pranks we
played,
All have since been put a stop-to by the naughty Board of
Trade;
The schooners and the merry crews are laid away to rest,
A little south the sunset in the Islands of the Blest.

John Masefield

THE FEMALE SMUGGLER

With her pistols loaded she went on board,
By her side hung a glittering sword,
In her belt two daggers – well arm'd for war
Was the Female Smuggler, who never feared a scar.

Anon.

THE ROGUE'S NIGHTMARE

One who, the self-same morning, had decoyed
The widow and her son with glozing talk,
At eve through springing pastures walked abroad,
And, after his poor sort, enjoyed his walk.
That night he dreamed: fresh flowers and April grass
Smothered his cruel pen; the white lamb kneeled
Upon his crafty parchments, signed and sealed
By victim hands; a babbling stream did pass
Sheer through those written wiles, till that base ink,
Which robb'd the widow's mite, the orphan's dole,
Lost colour. But that dream-begotten blink
Of damage waked at once his mammon-soul;
From his keen glance all vernal tokens shrink
While Fraud and Twilight watch the lying scroll.

Charles Tennyson-Turner

from THE SONG OF THE CARRION CROW

My roost is the creaking gibbet's beam,
   Where the murderer's bones swing bleaching;
Where the chattering chain rings back again
   To the night-wind's desolate screeching.

I have fluttered where secret work has been done,
   Wrought with a trusty blade;
But what did I care, whether foul or fair,
   If I shared the feast it made?

I plunged my beak in the marbling cheek,
   I perched on the clammy brow,
And a dainty treat was that fresh meat
   To the greedy Carrion Crow.

Far and wide is my charnel range,
   And rich carousel I keep,
Till back I come to my gibbet's home,
   To be merrily rocked to sleep.

When the world shall be spread with tombless dead
   And darkness shroud all below,
What triumph and glee to the last will be
   For the stateless Carrion Crow!

Eliza Cook

CLAUDE DUVAL

Born in Normandy, Claude Duval travelled to England in 1660 and as a highwayman became famous for his gentlemanly manners. So great was his reputation that when he was finally caught and hanged in 1670, many fashionable ladies wept over his body, which was on display. He received a splendid funeral at St Paul's Covent Garden, where he was buried beneath this epitaph.

Here lies Duval. Reader, if Male thou art,
Look to thy purse: if female, to thy heart.
Much havoc has he made of both, for all
Men he made stand, and women he made fall.
The second Conqueror of the Norman race,
Knights to his arms did yield, and Ladies to his face.
Old Tyburn's Glory: England's illustrious thief,
Duval, the Ladies' joy; Duval, the Ladies' grief.

Anon.

VILLON'S STRAIGHT TIP TO ALL CROSS COVES

'*Tout aux tavernes et aux filles.*'

Suppose you screeve? or go cheap-jack?
  Or fake the broads? or fig a nag?
Or thimble-rig? or knap a yack?
  Or pitch a snide? or smash a rag?
Suppose you duff? or nose and lag?
  Or get the straight, and land your pot?
How do you melt the multy swag?
  Booze and the blowens cop the lot.

Fiddle, or fence, or mace, or mack;
  Or moskeneer, or flash the drag;
Dead-lurk a crib, or do a crack;
  Pad with a slang, or chuck a fag;
Bonnet, or tout, or mump and gag;
  Rattle the tats, or mark the spot;
You can not bank a single stag;
  Booze and the blowens cop the lot.

Suppose you try a different tack,
  And on the square you flash your flag?
At penny-a-lining make your whack
  Or with the mummers mug and gag?
For nix, for nix the dibbs you bag!
  At any graft, no matter what,
Your merry goblins soon stravag:
  Booze and the blowens cop the lot.

The Moral

It's up the spout and Charley Wag
  With wipes and tickers and what not.
Until the squeezer nips your scrag,
  Booze and the blowens cop the lot.

W. E. Henley

A version of a poem by the French poet, Francois Villon (1431–?1462) which Henley told a friend he had 'blackguardized and initiated' . . . and said 'I shall leave you to find your way with a slang dictionary.' A translation may be found on page 174.

DEATH OF A GUNFIGHTER

Doc Holliday, who are you waiting for
With your fevered eyes alive?
Why do your hands feed cartridges
Into your pearl-handled forty-five?

Doc Holliday, why do you cock an ear
To the hoof beats pattering by?
Who is the stranger on a jet black mare
With death in either eye?

The room throbs like an oven,
The sun climbs up to noon,
The stranger sways in the rocking chair
Outside the Last Chance Saloon.

Doc Holliday asks for a mirror
No reflection in the glass
Only the ghosts of the men he's killed
Smiling as they pass.

The Pinkerton man in Ellsworth
When you were running from the law,
The kid in Dodge out to make his name
By beating you to the draw.

The breed in Butte, Montana,
Who marked you with that scar,
The dude who marked you with a slug in your thigh
From a face out in Wichita.

You can't be searching for glory now
For eternity in the sun
But hoping to find a kind of peace
In the mouth of a stranger's gun.

Doc Holliday white as the sheet on his bed,
The room about him reeled,
Coughed in his white bandanna
Stained like a poppy field.

The stranger sits quiet at the bedside
Watching the life blood spill
Doc's hands reach out for unseen guns
Then slowly flutter still.

The gun belt hangs on the bed post
The hat on a hook on the wall
And the high-heeled boots he'll never wear
Stand polished in the hall.

Doc Holliday died of tuberculosis in a sanatorium in Glenwood Springs at the age of thirty-five. On his death bed he is reputed to have asked for a last drink of whiskey, then raised his head, looked down at his feet and whispered, 'Well I'll be damned.' Doc had always sworn that he would die with his boots on.

Gareth Owen

— MY FRIEND MALONEY —

My friend Maloney, eighteen,
  Swears like a sentry,
Got into trouble two years back
  With the local gentry.

Parson and squire's sons
  Informed a copper.
The magistrate took one look at Maloney.
  Fixed him proper.

Talked of the crime of youth,
  The innocent victim.
Maloney never said a blind word
  To contradict him.

Maloney of Gun Street,
  Back of the Nuclear Mission,
Son of the town whore,
  Blamed television.

Justice, as usual, triumphed.
  Everyone felt fine.
Things went deader.
  Maloney went up the line.

Maloney learned one lesson:
  Never play the fool
With the products of especially a minor
  Public school.

Maloney lost a thing or two
   At that institution.
First shirt, second innocence,
   The old irresolution.

Found himself a girl-friend,
   Sharp suit, sharp collars.
Maloney on a moped,
   Pants full of dollars.

College boys on the corner
   In striped, strait blazers
Look at old Maloney,
   Eyes like razors.

'You don't need talent,' says Maloney.
   'You don't need looks.
All I got you got, fellers.
   You can keep your thick books.'

Parson got religion,
   Squire, in the end, the same.
The magistrate went over the wall.
   'Life,' said Maloney, ''s a game.'

Consider then the case of Maloney,
   College boys, parson, squire, beak.
Who was the victor and who was the
victim?
   Speak.

Charles Causley

A translation of Villon's 'Straight Tip to All Cross Coves' (p. 166) with thanks to R. K. R. Thornton

Suppose you write begging letters, or offer false bargains for sale,
Or work the three-card trick, or ginger a horse,
Or play the three-thimble trick, or steal a watch,
Or pass counterfeit money, or pass forged notes,
Suppose you palm off false goods as real, or grass and steal,
Or get a trustworthy tip and win a large sum,
How do you blow the blooming money?
Drink and the girls take it all.

Cheat, or receive stolen goods, or defraud, or pander,
Or pawn for more than something's worth, or wear women's clothing for immoral purposes,
Enter a dwelling during divine service, or commit a burglary,
Travel with a travelling show, or give someone a beating,
Act as a decoy at auctions, or look for custom, or beg and hoax,
Shake the (loaded) dice, or (? use marked cards),
You cannot bank a single shilling,
Drink and the girls take it all.

Suppose you try a different direction
And legitimately flaunt your medals (i.e. beg in uniform),
Be a literary hack to earn your money,
Or swindle and hoax with the players.
For nothing, for nothing the money you secure.
At any work, no matter what,
Your merry sovereigns soon abscond:
Drink and the girls take it all.

The Moral

Pawned and disappeared
Are handkerchiefs and watches and what not.
Until the hangman's noose pinches your neck,
Drink and the girls take it all.

ACKNOWLEDGEMENTS

The editor and publishers gratefully acknowledge the following for permission to reproduce copyright poems in this book:

'Flower Lover' by John Agard from *Shoot Me With Flowers*, published in 1973 by John Agard, copyright © John Agard, 1973, and 'One Question from a Bullet' by John Agard from *Mangoes and Bullets*, published by Pluto Press, 1985, copyright © John Agard, 1985, reprinted by kind permission of John Agard, c/o Caroline Sheldon Literary Agency; 'The Stuff' by Simon Armitage from *Zoom*, published by Bloodaxe Books, 1989, reprinted by permission of the publisher; 'Law Like Love' by W. H. Auden from *Collected Shorter Poems*, published by Faber & Faber Ltd, reprinted by permission of the publisher; 'The Tidy Burglar' by Leo Aylen from *Standpoints*, published by Harrap, 1983, and from *Rhymoceros*, published by Macmillan, 1989, copyright © Leo Aylen, 1983, reprinted by permission of the author; 'The Forger' and 'The Judge's Monologue' by Pranab Bandyopadhyay from *Call for Freedom* and *Whistles in the Wind*, published by United Writers, Calcutta, 1977 and 1978, copyright © Pranab Bandyopadhyay, 1977 and 1978, reprinted by permission of the author; 'The Borstal Boy' by George Barker from *Street Ballads*, published by Faber & Faber Ltd, reprinted by permission of the publisher; 'Burglary' by Taner Baybars from *To Catch a Falling Man*, published by Scorpion Press, 1963, copyright © Taner Baybars, 1963, reprinted by permission of the author; 'Peeping Tom' by Lois Beeson from *Ambit 127*, published by Ambit, 1992, copyright © Lois Beeson, 1992, reprinted by permission of the author; 'J Stands for James' and 'The Justice of the Peace' by Hilaire Belloc from *Complete Verse*, published by Pimlico, a division of Random House, reprinted by permission of Peters, Fraser & Dunlop; 'Charles Peace' by E. C. Bentley from *The Complete Clerihews of E. C. Bentley*, published by Oxford University Press, 1981, copyright © The Estate of E. C. Bentley, reprinted by permission of Curtis Brown Ltd, London, on behalf of the copyright owner; 'In-a Brixtan Markit' by James Berry from *A Chain of Days*, published by Oxford University Press, 1985, copyright © James Berry, 1985, reprinted by permission of Oxford University Press; 'The Arrest of Oscar Wilde at the Cadogan Hotel' by John Betjeman from *Collected Poems*, published by John Murray (Publishers) Ltd, reprinted by permission of the publisher; 'My Friend Maloney' and 'My Neighbour Mr Normanton' by Charles Causley from *Collected Poems* and *Figgie Hobbin*, published by Macmillan, reprinted by permission of David Higham Associates; '29' by Stanley Cook from *Form Photograph*, published by Peterloo Poets, 1976, copyright © Stanley Cook, 1976, reprinted by permission of the publisher; 'Yes, Officer' and 'Education for Leisure' by Carol Ann Duffy from *Standing Female Nude* and *Selling Manhattan*, published by Anvil Press, 1985 and 1987, copyright © Carol Ann Duffy, 1985 and 1987, reprinted by permission of the author; 'Wife Who Smashed Television Set Gets Jail' by Paul Durcan from *Teresa's Bar*, published by Gallery Press, 1976, copyright © Paul Durcan, 1976, reprinted by permission of Blackstaff Press; 'Last Suppers' by Sue Dymoke from *Hunting Ground*, published by Slow Dancer Press, 1992, copyright © Sue Dymoke, 1992, reprinted by permission of the author; from 'Trespassing' by Robert Frost from *Poetry of Robert Frost* edited by Edward Connery Lathen, published by Jonathan Cape, reprinted by permission of the publisher; 'On the Embankment' by Wilfred Gibson from *Collected Poems*, published by Macmillan London Ltd, reprinted by permission of the publisher; 'Shoplifting' by Mick Gowar from *Third Time Lucky*, published by Viking Kestrel, 1988, copyright © Mick Gowar, 1988, reprinted by permission of the publisher; 'Pocket Money' by Mick Gowar from *So Far So Good*, published by HarperCollins Publishers, 1986, reprinted by permission of the publisher; 'Convicted' by Jenny Hamlet, copyright © Jenny Hamlet, 1994, reprinted by permission of the author; 'Attila Takes a Hand' and 'Run' by Susan Hamlyn, copyright © Susan Hamlyn, 1994, reprinted by permission of the author; 'Bye-Child' by Seamus Heaney from *Wintering Out*, published by Faber & Faber Ltd, reprinted by permission of the publisher; 'Send for Lord Timothy' by John Heath-Stubbs from *Collected Poems*, published by Carcarnet, reprinted by permission of David Higham Associates; 'Local Mystery' by Stewart Henderson from *A Giant's Scrapbook*, published by Spire, 1989, copyright © Stewart Henderson, 1989, reprinted by permission of Hodder & Stoughton Publishers; 'Surprising Song of the King's Counsel' by A. P. Herbert from *A Book of Ballads*, reprinted by permission of A. P. Watt Ltd on behalf of Crystal Hale and Jocelyn Herbert; 'In the Can' and 'Strawberries' by Rosie Jackson, copyright © Rosie Jackson, 1994, reprinted by permission of the author; 'Warning to Parents' and 'A Coffee House' by Elizabeth Jennings from *Collected Poems*, published by Carcarnet, reprinted by permission of David Higham Associates; 'Dr Watson's Lament' by David King, copyright © David King, 1993, reprinted by permission of the author; 'Mute' by Lotte Kramer from *Pen International*, published by Pen, 1993, copyright © Lotte Kramer and *Pen International*, 1993, reprinted by permission of the author; Two poems from 'On Trial' – No. 8 'The Undecided' and No. 9 'The QCs' by Maurice Lindsay from *Requiem for a Sexual Athlete*, published by Robert Hale Ltd, 1988, reprinted by permission of the publisher; 'An Empty Phone Box' by Edward Lloyd, copyright © Edward Lloyd, 1994, reprinted by permission of the author; 'Brooklyn Cop' by Norman MacCaig from *Collected Poems*, published by

Chatto & Windus, 1990, copyright © Norman MacCaig, 1990, reprinted by permission of Chatto & Windus/Random House UK Ltd; 'The Ballad of John Silver' by John Masefield from *Salt Water Ballads*, published by Grant Richards, 1902, copyright © The Estate of John Masefield, 1902, reprinted by permission of the Society of Authors; 'Unlucky for Some' by Roger McGough from *Waving at Trains*, published by Jonathan Cape, reprinted by permission of Peters, Fraser & Dunlop; 'Man in Hotel Room with Stolen Fork' by Ian McMillan from *Tall in the Saddle*, published by Smith/Doorstop, 1986, copyright © Ian McMillan, 1986, reprinted by permission of the author; 'Behind the Stony' by Eric Millward from *Dead Letters*, published by Peterloo Poets, 1978, copyright © Eric Millward, 1978, reprinted by permission of the publisher; 'The Spoons' by Elma Mitchell from *Furnished Rooms*, published by Peterloo Poets, 1983, copyright © Elma Mitchell, 1983, reprinted by permission of the publisher; 'Playtime' by John Mole from *A Partial Light*, published by Dent, 1975, copyright © John Mole, 1975, reprinted by permission of the author; 'Four Seasons' by Hubert Moore from *Rolling Stock*, published by Enitharmon, 1991, copyright © Hubert Moore, 1991, reprinted by permission of the author; 'The Suspect' by Edwin Morgan from *Collected Poems*, published by Carcanet, reprinted by permission of the publisher; 'Eddy Scott Goes Out to Play' by David Orme, copyright © David Orme, 1994, reprinted by permission of the author; 'Death of a Gunfighter' by Gareth Owen from *Song of the City*, published by HarperCollins Publishers, reprinted by permission of the publisher; 'The Dorking Thigh' by William Plomer from *Country Ballads and Poems* and *Collected Poems*, published by Jonathan Cape, 1973, reprinted by permission of Random House UK Ltd; 'Fitting the Crime' by Peggy Poole, copyright © Peggy Poole, 1994, reprinted by permission of the author; 'The Victim Died of Stab Wounds' by F. Pratt-Green from *The Old Couple*, published by Peterloo Poets, 1976, copyright © F. Pratt-Green, 1976, reprinted by permission of the publisher; 'The Ballad of the Long Drop' by John Pudney from *Selected Poems*, published by J. M. Dent, 1973, reprinted by permission of David Higham Associates; 'To One in Prison' by Siegfried Sassoon, reprinted by permission of George Sassoon; 'Baby Dies in a Cupboard' by Carole Satyamurti, published by the magazine *Critical Survey*, 1992, and 'Sugar and Cream' by Carole Satyamurti, copyright © Carole Satyamurti, 1992 and 1994, reprinted by permission of the author; 'Uncle Albert' and 'A Case of Murder' by Vernon Scannell from *Mastering the Craft* and *Walking Wounded*, published by Pergammon Press and Eyre & Spottiswood in 1971 and 1965 respectively, copyright © Vernon Scannell, 1971 and 1965, reprinted by permission of the author; 'Prisoner and Judge' by Ian Serraillier from *I'll Tell You a Tale*, published by Kestrel, 1973, copyright © Ian Serraillier, 1973, reprinted by permission of Anne Serraillier on behalf of Ian Serraillier; 'We Don't Want It Grey' by Norman Silver from *Words on a Faded T-Shirt*, published by Faber & Faber Ltd, reprinted by permission of the publisher; 'Dare Devil' by Matt Simpson, copyright © Matt Simpson, 1994, reprinted by permission of the author; 'Eddy's Fire' by Valerie Sinason from *Inkstains and Stilettos*, published by Headland, 1986, copyright © Valerie Sinason, 1986, reprinted by permission of the author; 'Brady at Saddleworth Moor' by Ken Smith from *The Heart, The Border*, published by Bloodaxe Books, 1990, reprinted by permission of the publisher; 'Bag Snatching in Dublin' and 'From My Notes for a Series of Lectures on Murder' by Stevie Smith from *The Collected Poems of Stevie Smith*, published by Penguin 20th Century Classics, 1975, copyright © James MacGibbon, 1937, reprinted by permission of James MacGibbon; 'Young Thieves' and 'The Man Who Finds His Son has Become a Thief' by Raymond Souster from *Collected Poems Vol. 1* and *Vol. 2*, published by Oberon Press, 1980 and 1981, copyright © Oberon Press, 1980 and 1981, reprinted by permission of the publisher; 'Coroner's Jury' by L. A. G. Strong from *Collected Poems*, published by A. D. Peters Ltd, 1957, reprinted by permission of Peters, Fraser & Dunlop; 'A Holborn Lamppost' by Matthew Sweeney from *The Lame Walzter*, published by Allison & Busby, 1985, copyright © Matthew Sweeney, 1975, reprinted by permission of the author; 'Smart Boy' by A. S. J. Tessimond from *Voices in a Giant City*, published by Heinemann, 1947, and *The Collected Poems of A. S. J. Tessimond*, edited by Hubert Nicholson, published by Whiteknights Press, 1985, copyright © Tessimond's executor, Hubert Nicholson and his heirs, 1947, reprinted by permission of Whiteknights Press; from 'Under Milk Wood' by Dylan Thomas published by Dent, 1954, copyright © Trustees for the copyright of the late Dylan Thomas, reprinted by permission of David Higham Associates; 'I Used to Climb Up Lampposts, Sir' by Colin West from *Not to be Taken Seriously*, published by Hutchinson, 1982, copyright © Colin West, 1982, reprinted by permission of the author; 'Comeback' by Kit Wright from *Short Afternoons*, published by Hutchinson, 1991, reprinted by permission of Random House UK Ltd; 'Sergeant Brown's Parrot' by Kit Wright from *Rabbitting On*, published by HarperCollins Publishers, reprinted by permission of the publisher; 'Murder' by Yevgeny Yevtushenko from *Selected Poems*, translated by Robin Milner-Gulland and Peter Levi, published by Penguin Books, 1962, translation copyright © Robin Milner-Gulland & Peter Levi, 1962, reprinted by permission of the publisher; 'Hard' by Bernard Young, copyright © Bernard Young, 1994, reprinted by permission of the author.

Every effort has been made to trace copyright holders, but in a few cases this has proved impossible. The editor and publishers apologize for these cases of unwilling copyright transgression and would like to hear from any copyright holders not acknowledged.